ADVANCE PRAISE FOR
OVERCOMING THE MOM-LIFE CRISIS

"This book is perfect for women who feel overwhelmed and stressed out by the demands of parenting and modern life. It is a simple, step-by-step guide for prioritizing real self-care while continuing to care for kids and all of the other responsibilities. It is a blueprint to cultivate inner peace and happiness, which is a win/win for everyone!"

—Terri Cole, Psychotherapist, Founder of
Terri Cole's Real Love Revolution™ &
Terri Cole's Boundary Bootcamp™

Overcoming the MOM-LIFE CRISIS

DITCH THE GUILT,
PUT YOURSELF ON THE TO-DO LIST,
AND CREATE A LIFE YOU LOVE.

NINA RESTIERI

Post Hill
PRESS

A POST HILL PRESS BOOK
ISBN: 978-1-64293-721-3
ISBN (eBook): 978-1-64293-722-0

Overcoming the Mom-Life Crisis:
Ditch the Guilt, Put Yourself on the To-Do
List, and Create A Life You Love
© 2021 by Nina Restieri
All Rights Reserved

Cover design by Heather Harris

Post Hill Press
New York • Nashville
posthillpress.com

Published in the United States of America
1 2 3 4 5 6 7 8 9 10

To Andrew, Jenna, Matthew, and Jamie:
you are my sun, my moon, and all my stars.

—*E. E. Cummings*

TABLE OF CONTENTS

NOTE TO READER

*T*his story is factually accurate to the best of my recollection. Still, at times, I've changed a name, or a situation, or been intentionally vague. Some characters in this book are composites of a few different people.

I have tried to give credit where credit is due with the Resources section in the back of this book, doing my best not to inadvertently repeat an idea I'd heard or read elsewhere. To the best of my knowledge, what you're about to read is material gleaned from my own experience unless stated otherwise.

In the interest of keeping things simple, I've chosen to use terms like *mom, dad, she,* and *he,* but I wrote this book for everyone who feels overwhelmed by the demands of parenting, regardless of gender identity.

INTRODUCTION

If you don't like the road you're walking,
start paving another one.

—DOLLY PARTON

I huddled under the covers in my king-size bed, sniffling into a wadded tissue from the nightstand. I pulled the sheet all the way up so it covered my face. In the darkness of my bedroom so close to midnight, I tried not to make a sound so as not to wake the kids. The house trembled for a moment when the garage door opened and then closed downstairs; then I heard the dull, familiar thud of Larry's footsteps as he walked to the fridge to find his dinner.

Don't cry. Don't cry. Don't cry. You're a strong, powerful woman, always in control. I hoped that if I repeated this enough, eventually I'd start to believe it.

It had been an unremarkable day in my life. It was 2009 and like every day before that, as a mom of four young children, I'd done all the things I was supposed to do. Poured the Frosted Flakes into bowls and added the milk. Wiped up the dribbles and splashes that got all over the table. Lined up the bowls, plates, and cups in the dishwasher. I pushed the kids' sneakers onto their feet. Slid their backpacks over their arms. Held their hands to help them climb into the waiting minivan. I dropped them off with hugs and kisses at their four different schools in four different parts of town. I sat bundled up on the sideline at soccer practice, rushed into the grocery store to pick up a chicken to roast, got it into the oven just in time to start homework. Then baths and stories, snuggles and goodnight kisses.

I was proud of my momming. I gave the kids everything I had. Every. Single. Day.

As I heard Larry enter the room, I prayed he'd believe I was asleep and that no one would wake up asking for a glass of water or, worse, *another* story. I had nothing, absolutely nothing, left to give. This had become an increasingly regular feeling—being depleted simply by the day-to-day.

On some level, I was angry with myself for feeling that way. Who was I to feel sorry for myself? What nerve did I have? I was *lucky*, married for almost fifteen years to a kind, loving man, living in our beautiful home, with healthy kids. I knew better than to be ungrateful. Andrew, Jenna, Matthew, and Jamie were my world. Larry's income more than supported us, and I had the freedom to start my own business and build it at my pace, which I had done a few years earlier. Everyone was happy and well-adjusted. On the surface, everything about my suburban life was the stuff of those enviable family scenes I had watched so often in rom-com films.

So why was I hiding under the covers? Why the uncontrollable, daily tears? Why did I frequently find myself locked in my room, or driving in my car with my heart palpitating, or sitting on the couch with my kids, heart racing, unable to take a full, deep breath?

What was wrong with me? It's not like I was in a war zone. I was a stay-at-home mom in suburban Connecticut. How hard could that be?

Despite all the good in my life, I frequently found myself on the verge of collapse. My mind raced with unfounded, irrational fears, especially late at night. Publicly and on paper, I was a great mom, a loving wife, an overachieving "mom entrepreneur." Behind that mask I'd become a high-functioning mess, perpetually overwhelmed, sad, and anxious.

Epiphany by a Thousand Needles

Knowing I needed help with my mounting anxiety in the face of simple day-to-day tasks, I took the first baby step on what would become a years-long quest for inner peace. I eventually sought out many different remedies, modalities, and healers. Jacques, an acupuncturist and Chinese medicine doctor, was the first.

Acupuncture seemed like an easy way to reduce what I thought was standard mom overwhelm. My plan was to lie on the table and be fixed—that's how I thought it worked.

I didn't anticipate having to put any emotional honesty into acupuncture.

I didn't know whom I expected to meet the first time I walked into my acupuncturist's clinic, but it definitely wasn't Jacques. He strode into the treatment room wearing khakis, horned-rim glasses, and a Vineyard Vines button down—the *Dude* uniform of suburban Connecticut—looking like someone I could have gone to college with. I went to Colgate University, a small, liberal-arts bastion of preppy style. As it turned out, he went there too, though he'd graduated a few years before me. Despite looking like he'd just come from a business-casual lunch at the country club, Jacques was a practicing Buddhist and healer.

It was a strangely stark room, sparsely furnished with a couple of folding chairs and a table. He placed a plastic office chair in front of me and looked into my eyes. His eyes were brown, surrounded by soft crinkles. Though he'd just entered the room only a moment before, he was totally *there* with me.

He reached out for my hand, closed his eyes, and felt my pulse. First one hand, then the other. Then he opened his eyes and asked if he could look at my tongue.

As I stuck out my tongue, he took a look and started shaking his head. "You're totally overwhelmed," he said. "Overwhelmed and sad."

Don't cry. Don't cry. Don't cry.

I felt totally exposed. Although Jacques was simply evaluating my health from a clinical standpoint, he did so in a way that felt like he was really *seeing* me. Was I so deprived of emotional engagement that any hint of it, even in the clinical environment of a doctor's office, felt like a tidal wave of feeling within my body? Did I even want to be seen? I had gotten myself there to his office seeking help, but suddenly being faced with what might have prompted that need and what was causing it in the first place made me want to run.

As the truth of Jacques's words screamed in my gut, I felt heat rising up into my face. My eyes started to well up, and I willed myself to keep it together. I resisted the urge to flee. He let me cry for a few minutes, and talk a bit, until I finally I got up on the table for my treatment.

After that first appointment, Jacques's prescription, aside from weekly sessions with needles in my body, was to examine what wasn't working in my life and to either change it or accept it.

He wanted me to find my own happiness in the life I'd built. But how could I look inward for happiness when I could barely get through the day?

At first, all I could find was the other side of the equation: the struggle. I had built a beautiful, full life, but my days were filled with constant activities revolving around our kids. Taking care of them, in addition to my husband, our home, and everything else on my to-do list, took every ounce of my energy, leaving me depleted. There was always so much to do, and it felt like there was never a moment to relax or breathe. My shoulders were perpetually up by my ears, my jaw and hands always clenched. And if I did happen to have a moment to myself, I felt guilty about it, as though unproductivity of any kind was simply unacceptable. Everything fell to me, from breakfast to school to sports to errands to laundry to dinner prep to cleaning up. As a result, I was cranky and irritable with the kids, and my relationship with my husband had flatlined.

I simply wasn't strong enough to carry it all on my own any longer.

Why I Wrote This Book

After that first, fateful visit with Jacques, I started ever so slowly to right my ship.

Years and years, a multitude of therapists, coaches and healers, and hundreds of self-help books later (oh, and spoiler alert: one divorce), I climbed out of my dark, unhappy hole. I will never say "I'm fixed," as life is a constant work in progress. But, more than a decade after getting started, I'm happy.

I put my own needs on the to-do list and put myself back in the equation. I'm writing this book to tell you that *it feels great*. What's more, everyone around me is better for it.

Talking to other moms over the years made me realize I wasn't alone in my struggles. Overwhelm was the norm. Guilt was rampant. Even with all we did, it never felt like enough.

Who had time to sit back and enjoy the fruits of our efforts? And who had the "right" to feel unhappy? Knowing I wasn't alone helped me feel better.

I learned that stress doesn't merely sit in our minds. We carry it in our bodies. And if we let go, we fear our whole world will come crashing down. Everything, it seems, depends on keeping it together. Perfection for moms feels like the only option, or our kids will be messed up.

Like me, many of the women I spoke with didn't see a way out either. They were overwhelmed, stressed out, and unhappy, but didn't see a solution. And even the thought of prioritizing themselves seemed selfish and likely to be ineffective.

What these women were not understanding, and what with a lot of work I had come to know to be true, was that their misery was not only not good for them, but also not good for marriages. Not good for kids. Not good for anyone. Many moms think we're doing everyone a favor by sacrificing ourselves. We think we're doing what's best for our kids and our families. As it turns out, the opposite is true. Putting ourselves last is bad for our kids, our relationships, and ourselves.

In 2016, I distributed a survey to one hundred of my customers. The findings were startling.

✧ 80 percent felt overwhelmed.

✧ 95 percent felt stressed out.

✧ 80 percent struggled with managing time.

✧ 60 percent worried about being a good-enough mom.

✧ 80 percent struggled with finding time to take care of themselves.

✧ 65 percent struggled with feelings of guilt.

✧ Only 45 percent felt they had work-life balance.

Think about that: more than 95 percent were stressed out. It was basically unanimous.

With these stats on my mind, I realized all of my inner work and struggles suddenly had a purpose. That purpose was to help other people. And that's what this book is—my attempt to share what I learned. I want to give moms everywhere the most effective tools I know of to make the changes that lead to a happier and more beautiful life.

Overcoming the Mom-Life Crisis

It took me years of trial and error to discover what worked and what didn't, but *you* won't have to endure those years of trial and error because I've come up with a system to help you get through it. In the pages that follow, I'm going to share with you how I overcame my *mom-life crisis,* and help you beat yours with a step-by-step process.

Each chapter reveals an important moment in my life and the story that led to a breaking point or a turnaround. It's not a full chronology of my life, by any means, rather quick snapshots, stories, or circumstances that felt universally relatable to other moms out there reading.

To make it easy and faster for you, I've included not only the steps to success with real, actionable solutions, but lots of exercises at the end of each chapter to help you move through this process with ease. To work through the steps along the way, buy yourself a notebook or journal that you can use to complete the exercises in this book.

Be honest with yourself when completing the exercises. I spent a lot of years telling myself that everything was fine because it was too painful to face the fact that everything was *not at all fine*. Don't make the mistake I made! You'll only be cheating yourself.

I'm sharing my journey with you because I don't want you to experience what I went through. I don't want you hiding from your spouse and kids, crying under the covers.

The information I gathered as I worked through my own process was, to me, revolutionary. It took me years to undo all the old conditioning that made me constantly put myself last.

Once I learned to integrate my own needs into my to-do list, everything changed. I no longer hide from my feelings. I live authentically now. I know that my family functions better when I have a voice in it, so I speak my truth. I understand on a deep level that my needs and my voice matter as much as everyone else's.

That's what this book is about: overcoming the mom-life crisis and putting your needs back on the *to-do* list so you can create a life you love. Because I truly believe that our kids thrive when we're thriving. Our relationships with our partners thrive when we're thriving. You cannot give from an empty tank. But when your tank is full, it will run over with love and joy for everyone in your life—including yourself.

The biggest favor you can do for yourself, your kids, your partner, and your entire family is to commit, today, to taking care of you. Let's start putting your needs on the to-do list *in pen* and treating yourself with as much love and care as you give your children.

Chapter 1

AWARENESS

You are here not to shrink down to less,
but to blossom into more of who you really are.

—O*PRAH* W*INFREY*

"*M*ommmmmaaaa."

Feverish, a mist of sweat on his forehead, Jamie whimpered as I sat beside him, where he was lying on the couch in our living room. Always a snuggler, he shifted his weight toward me and nuzzled his face into my arm, then his tiny arms reached out for a glass of water on the table.

"Could we pway Monopowy one moah time?"

At age six, Jamie still couldn't pronounce his Rs or his Ls, but I couldn't get enough of his sweet little baby voice and adamantly refused to take him to a speech therapist.

Monopoly. Again. "Of course, honey!"

Monopoly had started to monopolize my life.

It was fall of 2010, and the notorious swine flu had the world melting down with fear. In the wake of the utter devastation and suffering of COVID-19, the relatively tame swine flu seems almost cute. But at the time, it was no joke, and it paid a lengthy visit to our home.

I put down my BlackBerry and feigned enthusiasm for another round, even though I was in the middle of writing an email I really needed to get to my business partner, Maureen. She'd been so patient with me while I'd been out of the office staying home with sick kids. Jamie sat up and picked the board game up off the floor, where we'd left it after we'd finished our last game a couple of hours earlier. I secretly hoped he'd lose interest after a few laps around the board, as was his usual pattern, so I could finish up the email.

Three of my kids came down with this brutal strain of the virus, one after another. It was kind of like the chicken pox: They didn't all get it at the same time—one infected the other and the next started to feel sick two weeks later, and so on. And so on. So Matthew had it first, then two weeks later Jenna got it, and then two weeks later Jamie got it as well.

The kids were sick for a total of six weeks. That's 60,480 straight minutes of brewing tea, making chicken soup, cleaning up vomit, playing Monopoly, watching TV, reading stories, doing laundry, playing cards, and playing board games we forgot we had. It's 1,008 hours of being cooped up inside the house, which seemed to get smaller and stuffier over the course of those hours. I rarely left, except for more supplies at the drugstore. I'd savor the short walk from the front door of my house to the car on a crisp October evening, feeling fresh oxygen fill my lungs as I stepped briefly away from the constant demands that were calling me at home.

Rock bottom had officially arrived.

Not What I Signed Up For

Having my own company gave me the freedom to work from anywhere, anytime. Not only could I stay connected with my phone and laptop, I didn't have a boss to protest my lack of focused, in-office face time. I could conduct meetings on the sidelines of the soccer field during Matt's practice, make calls while sitting in the carpool line, and pick color swatches with our production manager while watching the kids take swim lessons at the local pool. Initially, it made perfect sense that I'd continue to be on double duty, both working and raising the kids. I chose that for my life.

But there was a lot of time to think during the flu period. Mostly, I started thinking that this situation was not exactly what I had in mind when I set up this flexible work arrangement. I'd be carrying my sixteenth load of laundry of the week and catch myself thinking, *Why the hell is it always me doing the grunt work?*

I started to wonder why it was that when the kids were sick, I was always the one to stay home with them. Don't get me wrong, I wanted to be there. But why was there never even so much as a conversation about it? Because after six weeks of being the one home, with no break, it was getting seriously old.

In fact, why was it that I'd attended every parent-teacher conference alone? Why was I the only one who knew the names of our kids' teachers? Why was it that I cooked for the family every night? Why was it that I was the only one home for drop-off, pickup, dinner, and bedtime? Why was I the one who emptied the dishwasher, made the school lunches, bought the birthday presents, booked the dinner reservations, swept the floor, dropped off the clothes at the dry cleaners?

My husband wasn't intentionally MIA. He was simply focused on other things—mostly, on working hard and providing for us. When I'd ask for help at home, he wouldn't place the same importance on it that I did. What I viewed as necessary tasks to keep the household running smoothly, he viewed as valuable but not super important. Why take out the garbage when it's not overflowing? Why throw in the laundry today, when tomorrow is coming and there will undoubtedly be more dirty clothes? He knew the kitchen would be cleaned eventually. Why did it have to happen at that very second?

Somewhere along the way, we fell into a pattern of me asking him to help, him doing things his way, and me subsequently resenting him, wiping down the countertop with the tears clouding my eyes because *I always end up doing everything in this stupid house and it's not fair.*

By the time the flu hit, my resentment and self-pity were starting to snowball. Like with previous moments of stress and pending breakdown, I'd feel guilty and ungrateful and beat myself up because Larry was doing his best and working hard and providing for us and also *I chose this*. I no longer had any sense of what was reasonable and what wasn't, because by this point I was angry about everything. I was starting to go into victim mode, feeling sorry for myself and blaming him for my misery. It was a messy ball of feelings wrapped in a lot of self-loathing.

Larry and I were a progressive couple, and we were both committed to raising great kids. It was logical, therefore, that I'd always envisioned us holding hands in the sunshine with our four kids, equal partners and friends and lovers and household-duty sharers.

The truth was that we'd become less and less connected over time. I was resentful that for years I'd shouldered what seemed like the entire burden of childcare, household work, and emotional labor, while he went off to work each day, not coming home most nights until after the kids were in bed. My happiness had taken a nosedive in recent years, as our unhealthy and, as I saw them, unfair patterns became more and more the norm.

Here's the thing: It wasn't Larry's fault. I had willingly put myself in this position. *I chose this.*

But how had it gone so wrong?

Emotional Labor

Despite progress in terms of gender equality and a culture that increasingly celebrates "hands-on" dads, women still do 65 percent of the child-care work in households. That's according to a 2019 opinion piece by Darcy Lockman in the *New York Times*. What I eventually learned, post-swine-flu-rock-bottom, was an awareness of the *emotional labor* that goes into taking care of a family.

Gemma Hartley talks about emotional labor in her 2018 book, *Fed Up: Emotional Labor, Women, and the Way Forward*.

"Emotional labor," wrote Hartley, "as I define it, is emotion management and life management combined. It is the unpaid, invisible work we do to keep those around us comfortable and happy."

It's calling the school when someone's going to be out sick, keeping track of the doctor and dentist appointments, and taking the kids to the annual and sick visits. It's being the one who notices that one of the kids needs a winter coat and mittens, and then going out and buying them. It's keeping the laundry going, picking up the prescriptions, and keeping the fridge stocked with everyone's favorite foods. It's walking the dog, changing the litter box. It's managing the family calendar.

Emotional labor also includes being the one who remembers everything. The first words and first steps and first days of school, the dates of the extended family members' birthdays, and getting the holiday card photo taken. Someone has to remember the kids' shoe sizes and small things like running low on laundry detergent and needing to pick up more, or knowing that the only vegetable Jamie will eat willingly is cauliflower. The emotional labor bearer makes endless lists to track things to keep the household running smoothly.

Emotional labor is also being the one who's highly attuned to everyone's emotions. It's being highly empathic, feeling what the kids are feeling, being heartbroken when they're sad and elated when they're happy. You're the one who notices your kids' emotional ups and downs. You sense when Andrew's unhappy at school or when Jenna's fighting with her best friend. You feel it intuitively when Matt needs some extra love and make a mental note to provide extra cuddles at bedtime. It's carrying the weight of the kids' sadness on your own shoulders, feeling like you somehow make their load lighter when you carry it with them.

Emotional labor, while time- and energy-consuming, is almost always invisible, unpaid, and unappreciated. It's emotionally exhausting. But as all of us who do it know, the household would fall apart without it.

My epiphany, while my kids were home with the flu, was that it wasn't just work and raising kids that were hitting me hard and causing strain in my marriage...it was also the emotional labor that went along with those two jobs.

Water, Slowly Reaching a Boil

When I met Larry in 1993, we were both recent college graduates establishing our independence in New York City. Larry was in grad school, and I worked at an advertising agency. With Larry and me, it was an easy relationship, not only because we had similar backgrounds from Italian-American families, but because we both wanted the same things, marriage and a family. We married within two years of meeting and moved to suburban Connecticut.

Our first child, Andrew, came quickly, followed soon after by Jenna, Matthew, and Jamie. I fell madly in love with my kids, beyond anything I'd ever experienced. I loved their delicious soft skin, the smell of their breath, their tiny hands holding a crayon to draw a picture, the way my baby Jamie would close his eyes and nuzzle his face into my neck.

Larry started working on Wall Street, and I eventually stopped working so I could stay home with the kids. I threw myself into the role of stay-at-home-mom and home manager, applying my type-A tendencies to everything from preschool admissions to home renovations to dinner preparation. I felt a deep sense of contentment as a mom, but I was lonely. Larry seemed to be at work all the time, and his job was an hour-and-a-half commute from our home in Connecticut. He was a great dad and on weekends, when he was home from work, he was a totally hands-on, pancake-making, sports-coaching, 24/7 dad. But during the week, I was essentially on my own.

To be completely transparent, I want to acknowledge that I did have help. Our nanny, Cicely, was like my right arm at home, always there to back me up by staying home with Jamie or doing the laundry while I was out driving the older kids around. I have only gratitude for Cicely, as it was because of her that I had the freedom to start my company.

When I started *momAgenda*, the kids were seven, five, three, and one. As much as I loved being a mom to my kids, I missed working. But I didn't want to lose my ability to be the mom I wanted to be. I didn't want to have a boss that could tell me I had to be somewhere at a particular time. I didn't want to miss important milestones in my kids' lives because of some outside force that I had no control over. The answer was to start my own company. That way I wouldn't lose the freedom to bring the kids to school, pick them up, show up for them at sporting events, and chaperone the field trips. Setting up an office right down the street from home and school meant I could be in either place at a moment's notice. I envisioned working each day while the kids were in school and then picking up the kids and going home, ready for full-time mom mode.

But the business quickly took off, surprising everyone, most of all me. What started as my little side project soon became a full-time occupation. I'd doubled my responsibilities, almost overnight.

You know that story about the frog in the hot water? The poor little guy thinks he's taking a bath. He doesn't even realize he's getting boiled because the water gets hot so gradually, until all of a sudden it's so hot that the frog can no longer survive.

I had jumped into the water and hung out there for years, as it got warmer and warmer, until my kids got the flu. And in that moment, I knew I wasn't just in hot water—it was scalding me. I'd been so busy that I'd abandoned any semblance of self-care, and fallen into a major physical, emotional, and spiritual funk. In the absence of anything that might have sustained my sanity and wellness, I turned to empty, unhealthy coping mechanisms that felt good in the moment but didn't actually benefit me. These guilty pleasures were my lifeline, providing much-needed, short-term doses of pleasure when I needed them.

Those pleasures had consequences. I gained more than thirty pounds since my wedding. Every night I cooked rich, decadent meals for my family, like pasta drowning in creamy sauce with butter-soaked garlic bread on the side. I baked homemade bread, oatmeal chocolate chip cookies, and double-chocolate brownies, the yummy fragrances filling the house, the flavors providing comfort and pleasure. "I know I shouldn't," I would tell myself. "But I *deserve* a treat," I'd say, as I filled another bowl of pasta carbonara, crisp bacon fat glistening on top.

I drank at least two or three glasses of pinot noir each night with dinner. "Just for tonight," I'd tell myself as I poured another glass, despite the fact that I found myself in this situation most nights of the week. Drinking softened the edges of my feelings. I had dinner with my kids every night, but Larry often didn't get home until after the kids were in bed. I missed him and the feeling of having dinner as a family, and wine made it more bearable.

One night my friend Susan asked my son Andrew, who by then was around twelve, "What's your mom's favorite food?" Andrew replied, his voice filled with sass, "Pinot noir." "That's not a food!" my friend exclaimed. Andrew rolled his eyes. "To my mom, it is."

The addition of my business meant I was constantly hurrying to meetings, driving the kids to their various schools and extracurriculars, running errands, or staying busy at the office, never stopping to breathe. The minute I slowed down I felt guilty that I wasn't doing something more "important." The truth was, I didn't really like to slow down, because when I slowed down I'd start thinking, and that would lead me to a darker place.

Although I took an antidepressant each day for the mild depression that had been with me for most of my life, and despite the additional self-medication with food, alcohol, and shopping, my anxiety levels were rising. In an alarming development, I started to have trouble breathing, not just while working out but simply sitting on the couch, trying to enjoy time with my kids.

I searched the internet and imagined all sorts of fatal medical conditions, but it turned out after consulting with doctors, my breathing problems were caused by anxiety. I added Xanax to the fix-list, and took it almost every night as an accompaniment to my multiple glasses of pinot noir. I panicked when my psychopharmacologist suggested I limit my Xanax ingestion to four nights per week. Didn't he know there were seven nights and I needed my Xanax every one of them? After a long day of kids and work and laundry and cooking and driving and everything else I did, I really looked forward to an evening with that feeling of floating in a soft, happy, blurry haze until I fell asleep.

Worst of all, my relationship with Larry was in shambles. In the span of just a few years we had become roommates who rarely had a moment of closeness. While I'd thrown myself into parenting four young kids and building my business, he'd thrown himself into his dream job as a budding Master of the Universe on Wall Street. We were living side-by-side, parallel lives, no longer intertwined like a couple, lacking even a semblance of intimacy between us.

There I was, lonely, overwhelmed, overweight, and over-medicated, and believing I had no right to feel so sad.

The Mom-Life Crisis: Seeking Help

"I'm in a funk," I told my friend Nancy over Cobb salad (her) and ravioli with cream sauce (me) at our favorite local lunch spot. Nancy had a thriving career as a therapist and was my go-to for mental-health advice. "Everything's great but I'm not happy. I think I'm having a midlife crisis."

Nancy shook her head. "It's not a midlife crisis. It's a *mom*-life crisis," she said. "It happens when you take care of everyone else all the time. You're frustrated and exhausted and anxious and emotionally drained because you're so busy and overwhelmed with kids and everything else that you've stopped taking care of yourself."

"You need to see Sherry," Nancy replied. "She's my mentor. She's in the city and she's expensive, but she goes deep. She's the best."

I wasn't thrilled about going to see a therapist in the city. After 9/11, visiting my once-beloved New York made me anxious. I'd started avoiding it, just as I'd started avoiding airplanes, bridges, and tunnels, among other things, gradually allowing my world to shrink.

Plus, I didn't have the time to add yet another thing to my to-do list.

Nancy sensed my hesitation. "I know she's the right one for you. Just trust me?"

Nancy was right. Before the ship went down completely, I needed to get help. I was too deep into my darkness to see light.

A few weeks later, I knocked on the door of a first-floor, pre-war apartment in an elegant building on Manhattan's Upper West Side. Sherry welcomed me into a one-room office decorated in tasteful shades of gray. She was older, rail-thin, and impeccably dressed in neutral shades. Her painted nails were the perfect shade of coral; her strawberry-blonde hair arranged in an elegant bun.

I felt ungainly and awkward, like a schlub sitting on her couch with my extra thirty pounds and my too-small jeans, enduring the discomfort of my muffin top flowing over my waistband. Sherry looked like she'd never exceeded a size two.

I felt ashamed as I sat there—of my unhappiness, my weight, my drinking, my Xanax. I was ashamed that my relationship with my husband was so empty. Why didn't I have close relationships with anyone other than my children? *What has happened to me?*

"What should we talk about today?" Sherry asked one day.

We'd gotten into the routine of weekly sessions. They had become my lifeline.

"I'm just so overwhelmed. I feel like I'm losing my mind," I said, before launching into a litany of how busy I'd been. I recounted my to-do list—activities that would further my kids' academic and extracurricular careers. It was exhaustive but felt surprisingly good to talk about. I was secretly proud of everything I was accomplishing in a day. I got a little ego boost when people said, "Wow! Your plate is really full!"

"That's quite a to-do list," Sherry said, nodding. "Very impressive. But I'm wondering where your needs are on that list."

My needs?

I sat, stunned and speechless. I'd honestly never thought about what I might need, beyond that second bowl of pasta or third glass of wine. I didn't consider my needs important enough to warrant a place on that to-do list.

"Don't you deserve to be a part of the equation?" she asked. "Don't you deserve as much love and care and consideration as your children?"

Don't cry. Don't cry. Don't cry.

"I don't have time for anything else," I said, hearing my voice shaking.

"You make your time," she said. "You decide what you do each day of your one, precious, beautiful life."

I sat as still as stone, letting her words sink in.

"Don't you want to make choices that make you happy?" she said.

There was that notion, again, that I first heard from Jacques—*my happiness.*

Put Your Own Oxygen Mask on First

Everyone's heard the airplane flight attendant say, "Put your own oxygen mask on first, then help others." But as moms, we tend to forget this advice and focus all our attention on others, depriving ourselves of the very air we need to survive and thrive.

This is how a mom-life crisis takes hold. And while some may dismiss our complaints, given that we're living relatively safe and privileged lives, the truth is that many moms are feeling like crap. And they feel guilty about that, too, which makes them feel even worse.

We take care of EVERYONE, from our kids to our spouses to our extended networks of family and friends—saying yes to everything that's asked of us because we feel guilty if we say no. We wear our "crazy busy" labels like badges of honor, trying to outdo each other with ever-increasing commitments and responsibilities. But our to-do lists are so packed that we can't possibly get it all done, so we feel like failures before we've even begun.

We fear letting others down. We worry we won't be liked. We're afraid people will talk behind our backs. There's an innate need for others' approval that drives us to say yes to things that make our to-do lists longer but don't help move us forward with our goals. We're only human—we want people to like us and see us as valuable.

Most of all, we want to be the best moms we can be, so we put our kids' needs first, often sacrificing our own needs for their happiness and well-being. For so many of us, our kids' happiness replaces our own, our boundaries having effectively disappeared.

What does it mean to put your oxygen mask on first? I went on a journey to find out. I read hundreds of books and articles; participated in workshops, seminars, and classes; and worked with a wide variety of different modalities of coaches and therapists. Each experience helped me gain awareness and led me bit by bit to understand what it meant and why it was important.

It means making the decision *that you matter*. It means prioritizing from the inside out so that your outer life reflects your personal priorities. It means saying no to commitments that aren't aligned with those priorities. It means giving yourself permission to do what you want to do—even if what you want to do is rest. It means placing greater focus on pleasure and happiness in your day-to-day life.

It means taking care of your *physical* self so that you feel your best. For example, you may need to prioritize sleep in order to get your full seven to eight hours per night. You may find you need a new eating plan that energizes you and makes you feel healthier. You may need a daily walk outside or a gym workout to feel energized and alive again.

It means taking care of your *emotional* self so that you can engage fully in relationships with yourself and others. Maybe you need to take time for therapy or journaling or meditation or making gratitude lists. Maybe you need a regularly scheduled date night with your partner or more time with your girlfriends. Maybe you need to engage more in your community to feel a sense of belonging...or maybe just the opposite—to disengage from the various committees you've joined and finally get some alone time.

It means taking care of your *social* self by eliminating toxic friendships that drain your energy and surrounding yourself with friends who push you to grow. It means taking care of your mental self by staying curious and always learning. And it goes beyond, to encompass every aspect of life.

You Are Not Alone

It's important for you to know that you're not alone, that the mom-life crisis is an epidemic among modern moms. It's also important to know that you haven't done anything wrong. Maybe your mom sacrificed herself for her kids, and that's the example you're subconsciously following. Or maybe you've internalized the message, like I did, that "good moms" sacrifice themselves to care for their families.

Part of the problem is letting other people's opinions into our minds. In fact, it's time for society as a whole to reject that idea, because generations of moms have suffered because of it for too long.

Some thoughts to consider:

✧ What would it feel like to nurture yourself with as much love, kindness, attention, and care that you'd give to your new baby?

✧ How would it feel to love yourself as much as you love your kids and your partner?

✧ What would it feel like to understand on a deep level that your happiness, your pleasure, your fun, and your health are just as important as that of your kids?

Discovering the answers to those questions begins with awareness. Moms are among the most underappreciated, underpaid, overworked members of our society. In many cases, we're expected to do the majority of the work to raise the kids and run the household, in addition to whatever job we may hold outside the home. Our happiness takes a big hit as a result of all this multitasking, as does our health—both mental and physical—despite the strides our society has taken in terms of gender equality.

Once we gain an awareness of the problem, we can start to change. Transformation begins on an individual level. Each one of us is responsible for making her own change happen— no one is going to do this work for us.

You'll likely get resistance at home and from judgmental outsiders once you start putting yourself on your to-do list. That's because, even today, it's revolutionary for any woman, but especially a mom, to stand up and declare that she's going to focus her energy not just on her kids and partner, but also on herself.

You'll even get resistance from a most unlikely source: yourself.

That's because you'll be upgrading the internal scripts and blueprints that were set in stone in childhood, and that doesn't happen overnight. It requires patience and practice. Some days, you'll fall back into your old patterns. That's okay—this journey is not a straight line. As Cheryl Strayed, author of *Wild*, has said: "Believe in the integrity and value of the jagged path."

Women can be biting in their criticisms of other women. We've all heard those women at the playground talking behind each other's backs, saying things like, "I can't believe she actually thinks she can have a life after having kids." That's why taking these steps is necessary for everyone. Spread the word! Once we're *all* experiencing the abundance of happiness and pleasure that comes when we put our own needs on the to-do list, we'll start to see each other with compassion and empathy rather than in competition.

Depriving ourselves makes us miserable, which makes us judge ourselves and everyone around us. Taking care of our needs leaves us fulfilled, happy—which leads to more love and support of everyone in our lives. I know which one I've chosen. For the rest of my life, I'm committed to taking care of my needs as well as I take care of the needs of my kids. I now know from experience that everyone in my life thrives when I'm at my best.

Now, it's time to take action. The first step to putting yourself on the to-do list is *awareness*. We're going to start by identifying where in your life you're depriving yourself. Where have you let your needs slide in the service of other people's needs?

Today's To-Dos: Awareness

Write answers to the following questions in your notebook.

First, rank each area of your life on a scale of 1 to 10, with 10 being awesome and 1 being unacceptable. Rank the following and add any others that apply:

Relationship with partner:

Connection with kids:

Relationship with self:

Emotional fulfillment:

Relationships with extended family:

Relationships with friends:

Leisure time pursuits:

Spiritual life:

Stress management:

Health:

Fitness:

Finances:

Career:

Physical surroundings, e.g., feeling comfortable in my home:

Overall mood:

Happiness overall:

Now, expand on the areas you ranked 7 or above.

What are you really happy about in your life right now?

Where in life do you feel fulfilled?

Where are your needs being met?

Why are these parts working so well?

Expand on the areas you ranked 6 or below.

What areas of your life are you not happy with at this time?

Where do you feel like you need to place more attention?

Chapter 2
SHOULDS

*Happiness comes from being who you actually are
instead of who you think you are supposed to be.*

—SHONDA RHIMES

"It's official. I'm having a mom-life crisis," I told my best friend, Heidi, one night over dinner.

We sat at a candlelit table at a tiny Italian restaurant in the East Village of Manhattan, having finally managed to figure out a night that worked for both of us amid our crazy schedules. The flu had come and gone in my house. Heidi worked full time in the city, and her two young sons played travel hockey, making it harder to make plans with her than just about anyone else I knew. It had taken weeks to nail down this dinner date.

"A midlife crisis? Aren't you a little young for that?" she asked.

"Not a midlife crisis," I corrected her. "A *mom*-life crisis."

Heidi shook her head, so I explained.

"It's not like a man's midlife crisis where you go out and buy a sports car and date twenty-five-year-olds," I told her. "It's when you do everything for everyone else and don't have time for yourself. My therapist says I need to start putting myself back on the to-do list."

"Ahhhhh," she nodded. "I mean, isn't that the case for basically everyone we know?"

Um, yeah. Heidi and I had gone to college together. It seemed like most, if not all, of our old friends were going through something similar.

"I know I keep saying this, but you really should try the studio," Heidi said. "Especially now. You need it."

Heidi had been trying to persuade me to take classes at her favorite pole dance studio for years. It had undeniably had an enormously positive impact on Heidi's life. She exuded health and radiance, not to mention maintaining her physical fitness, despite the grueling schedule she maintained and all the responsibilities she juggled. She had that glow from within, something I normally associate with people who practice yoga every day.

"They keep the studio dark, and there are no mirrors," she said, "so there's no judgment. It's not about looking hot or performing for others—it's about how you feel." Heidi explained that the pole dancing classes were a supportive, empowering environment, and the women are all ages and shapes and sizes. Everyone is accepted there. It's not even really about the pole dancing! It's about feeling confident and sexy and powerful again.

I gave my typical, often-repeated response for people who suggested I try new things. I could recite it in my sleep. "I mean, I'd love to, but I have four kids and a business. I barely have time to brush my teeth."

I'd always dismissed Heidi's attempts to get me to try it, using my hectic schedule as an excuse. But the truth was, I viewed the idea of pole dancing as highly suspect and potentially inappropriate. And the idea of *me* pole dancing was completely ridiculous and out of the question. It was fine for Heidi to do it—it was her life and her decision. But for me, it didn't feel like something a married mom of four should do.

Should.

At that period in my life, when making decisions, I didn't consider what might be best for me, or what might bring me joy, or what I might actually *want*. My decision-making criteria had nothing to do with my happiness and everything to do with my warped, outdated perception of what I thought I was supposed to do. I'd replaced independent thought with duty and obligation.

I *should* volunteer for the school fundraiser.

I *should* make a home-cooked meal each night.

I *shouldn't* wear that little dress.

I *should* get the salad.

I *should* go to the gym every day.

I *should* volunteer for the PTA.

In my desire to be a great mom, wife, and business owner, I'd lost my inner compass and replaced it with an externally based worldview that didn't reflect who I was or even what I wanted.

The word *should* had taken over my life.

Shoulds are dangerous that way. They sneak into your consciousness without you even realizing it. They shame you into submission, making you feel guilty and unsure of yourself. And they disempower you into making choices you don't want to make. How can you really enjoy the take-out meal when a little voice inside you is saying you should have cooked something at home, and that doing so would make you somehow better?

Sometimes shoulds are even bigger than making meatloaf, encompassing the most important decisions we'll make in life. These *big shoulds* are rules we subconsciously created a long time ago, as children, based on observations of our parents and other significant people who contributed to our upbringing. Each of us formulates our own list of big shoulds without realizing it. And then we become adults, and unless we completed lots of therapy or other personal growth work, we tend to make decisions that are based on what that young child observed all those years ago.

Classic examples include:

A mom should stay home with her kids rather than work.

A mom should sacrifice herself in order to care for her children.

A mom should go to work in the family business rather than pursuing her dream of becoming an actor/writer/rock star.

These shoulds are generally programmed into us at an early age. They're so ingrained that even if we know intellectually they're not true, they deviously mess with our minds and try to control our behavior.

Let me give you an example that might ring true to you. Let's say one of your shoulds is, "A mom should stay in at night with her kids, rather than hire a babysitter and enjoy a night out with her girlfriends."

In this example, you may have formed a perception at some point early in life that moms aren't supposed to go out and do fun things, that they should always be home and available for their kids. Maybe this idea came from observing your mom, who rarely took time for herself and never went out at night. You may not be consciously thinking about it, but the belief system is still operating in the back of your mind, whispering in your ear, making you feel guilty, and maybe even leading you to avoid the behavior altogether. In this way, shoulds can limit you and your potential enjoyment of life.

You likely have your own unique batch of shoulds operating right now in the back of your mind. These rules can be constricting, not to mention the fact that they're usually made by young, innocent, inexperienced versions of ourselves. As we mature into adults, these rules expand into limiting beliefs that keep us from doing the things that bring us joy. We miss out on having a full-spectrum life.

For example, if you grew up with a single mom who said things like, "You shouldn't ever trust or depend on a man," (which many of us growing up in the '70s and '80s heard) you've internalized that belief. (As a young child, you probably didn't question her statements—your survival depended on her, after all.) And then you grew up, with a tendency to avoid trusting men because of an observation you made when you were seven years old, based on the rants of someone who felt justifiably angry at her shitty ex-husband. But here's the thing: while what she said may have been how she felt in the moment, it wasn't true in the bigger picture, and now it's wrecking your relationships and possibly your life.

It's important to identify these thought patterns so the child you once were stops influencing the adult you are now. Isn't it time to make decisions that serve you?

It's also important because shoulds are a form of negative thinking, making you feel guilty and ashamed, and can lead to depression and anxiety. These thoughts can imprison you into a small life where you're afraid to venture out and try new things for fear of what others may think or the guilt you may impose upon yourself.

Sometimes, shoulds can be a good thing. As in, *I should get a pap smear each year*, or *I should include vegetables in my diet*. I'm not talking about those shoulds here. I'm talking about the ones that limit your life due to outdated ideas that were put in your head during childhood.

But how do you know the difference between healthy and unhealthy shoulds? It can be a fine line. One indicator: a should that leads to a quantifiably better result is usually a healthy should. So in the above example, it's now a well-researched fact that eating vegetables has a positive effect on a person's health, so that's a quantifiably better result than not eating vegetables. Whereas you can't quantify whether it's better for you to stay in or go out for a date night with your spouse—a valid argument could be made either way. So that's an unhealthy should.

Shooing the Shoulds

Eliminating shoulds begins with understanding them. These thoughts serve only one purpose: to imprison you and make you feel bad about yourself. That's why I recommend everyone eliminate the word *should* from their vocabulary and shift to a more empowered mindset.

Eliminating shoulds begins and ends with reframing. *Rather than doing what you think you "should" do, based on external influences or limiting beliefs, ask yourself what you really want.*

Let's say you're in an adorable little shoe store in Southampton, Long Island, with a friend and you've fallen in

love with a fabulous pair of shoes, a situation I found myself
in a few years ago. They were red and tan, high-heeled wedge
flip flops with a big flower on the top of the straps. So cute, so
fun, and so utterly impractical.

I shouldn't. My "should voice" started telling me all the
bad things that would happen if I bought the shoes. *It would
be irresponsible! I should spend any extra money on my kids! I
don't need new shoes, especially red flip flops!*

"Oh, come on! When was the last time you treated yourself?" my friend asked me that day.

I thought about what I really wanted. I hadn't shopped for
myself, or for anything other than kids' stuff, in ages. What I
really wanted in that moment was to treat myself to something
totally fun and just for me. The shoes were inexpensive and
wouldn't break the bank. And they represented what I really
wanted at that time—a fun and pleasurable treat for myself.

So, I bought the shoes.

Once I removed the should and thought about *what I
really wanted*, my perspective shifted, and I became empowered to do what was right for me based on my present-day
desires, rather than based on old, outdated scripts about
spending money.

If what I'd really wanted at that time in my life was more
money in my savings account, I would have made a different choice. And I would have felt totally empowered in that
choice as well.

If you remove the should in the above example, you'll find there are simply two different viewpoints, one of which will lead to you getting exactly what you want. You're completely empowered, in every decision you make, to think of the bigger picture of what you want and then decide.

So the next time you start to hear your own inner dialogue telling you what you should or shouldn't do, interrupt it. Tell that voice to quiet down…and then ask yourself *what you really want.*

Buying a pair of shoes was low-consequence. Ignoring a larger should that truly went against my predispositioned belief, that took some digging. I started by asking myself a simple question:

What do I really want?

The answer: *I want to feel like the old me again.*

Shoes weren't going to make me feel like myself. Therapy was helping. Acupuncture was helping. But I needed a shake-up to knock out a should that deep in my heart I knew needed to be ignored.

The pole dance studio. That was a big one.

After my dinner with Heidi, I finally made the decision to check it out. I was going to put my should aside for once and try something new, something that intrigued me, something I was afraid of, and mostly something I could think of no other reason to ignore except that dumb should.

Today's To-Dos: Shoulds

To eliminate the bad should you need to examine your subconscious patterns and limiting beliefs and figure out how they have impacted your life. Once you identify these patterns, you'll be operating from a place of awareness and strength, rather than allowing old beliefs to shape your current-day behaviors.

To-Do #1

Write down your should statements in your journal whenever they come up for you.

For example, "I should make a homemade meal each night for the kids."

Now try to reframe each should statement with a more empowered one.

For example, "I choose to feed my kids healthy foods, whether homemade, store-bought, or take-out."

To-Do #2

Write down these questions in your journal and fill in the blanks at the end with your answers. Write as much as you want in response to each statement.

A good mom should _____

A good mom should not _____

If I_____, people will _____

My kids should _____

My kids should not _____

My spouse/partner should _____

My spouse/partner should not _____

Other moms should _____

Other moms should not _____

If I could just _____, then I'd be happy

Chapter 3

THE MYTH OF THE "GOOD MOM"

This is one thing they forget to mention in most child-rearing books, that at times you will just lose your mind. Period.

—ANNE LAMOTT

I pressed my back up against the wall in the dark, hoping my lace-up stiletto boots wouldn't hit any of the battery-powered candles that were scattered around the floor. Red lamps glowed in the corners of the room, where five stainless-steel dance poles posed a stark contrast to the scarlet walls and the plush chairs in the corners. While the bass notes of the music filled the studio, I kept my back pressed against the wall and pushed my hips forward, starting to circle them slowly, eyes closed, head back. As my hands ran through my hair, pushing it over my eyes, I slowly moved my back down the wall, inch by inch, until I landed with a little thud on my ass, a tangled mess of bent limbs and hair and straps everywhere.

"Take up space," the teacher said. "Let your hips take up space…your hands…your whole being."

I rolled onto my belly on the purple mat on the floor and let my hips move in slow circles, grinding up in the air, then down against the floor. I involuntarily let out a moan. Taking up space was a welcome change from my everyday life.

I chose an introductory class at noon on a Friday in December, a few weeks after having dinner with Heidi. And I went back every single week for the next eight years.

It was nothing like what I expected, and all my shoulds turned out to be moot points. It was all women, of all ages and shapes, in an empowering, supportive environment, just like Heidi had said. And these women were dancing *for themselves—not for men or for anyone else.* It turned out to be exactly what I needed at that time in my life.

This dance studio had become the place where I could exhale with pure relief, let the world slip away, and lose track of time for hours. It was where I felt like I belonged. Where I could be sexy and sensual and angry and sad and soulful and naughty and big and provocative. I could stomp my stiletto boot in anger, or cry in the corner with deep, soulful sadness. I could strut around and feel like the hottest woman on the planet. Or I could cover myself up and hide under a silk scarf, too shy to be seen. I could fill the entire room with my being, no apologies necessary. I could be all of me here, the whole, messy, complex package. Week by week, I did all the above depending on the day and my mood.

I'd been searching my entire adult life for a form of exercise that I truly loved, that would make me lose track of time for hours and enter into a state of flow. I'd heard it said that, eventually, everyone finds their favorite physical activity, the one that really clicks and makes them want to return again and again. "It's like dating," friends told me. "Keep trying new things and eventually you'll find the right one." For some women, it's tennis; for others it's golf or running or Zumba. I'm not one of those women. For me, it's pole dancing.

You can imagine my confusion at discovering I'd finally found my happy place, my home, my tribe, and my community, and *it was dancing on a pole.* I'd tried running and aerobics and barre classes. I'd tried hot yoga and personal training and Pilates.

Why did it have to be pole dancing?

How could I be a good mom if pole dancing was my hobby?

Some people think of pole dancing as lurid. It's not. I respect women who do it professionally. Still, I was doing something different than the pros. I was taking a class, in a women-only dance studio, that allowed me to experience a type of movement that felt delicious and natural, like home to my body. But I was overwhelmed by the preconceived notions and what people would think.

I was raised to be a good Catholic girl, to behave appropriately. I was raised to dress modestly, drink moderately, and restrain my darker emotions like anger, sadness, and frustration, pushing them aside. To put a smile on my face and say, "I'm fine," even when I wasn't. To suppress my feelings if they got to be too big or threatened to make anyone uncomfortable. To deny my needs when they interfered with what would make everyone else in my life happy.

Not to mention, I was a *mom of four young children*. This was not how a good mom from the suburbs should behave!

Was it?

Still, I had put all that stuff aside. And I'm glad I did. I almost let the preconceived ideas that I'd formed in childhood, about what good moms should or shouldn't do, prevent me from experiencing something that added immeasurably to my life.

That didn't mean I escaped judgment from others.

Don't Abandon Yourself to Be a Good Mom

I'd fallen head-over-heels (literally) in love with the pole movement and actually *installed a stainless-steel dance pole in my home office.*

But I knew my new hobby wasn't going to play well among the other moms.

Early one Saturday morning, I was watching my youngest son, Jamie, play basketball. The mom sitting next to me,
Karen, was someone I knew casually through our kids. Her
son was a good friend of Jamie's. We weren't close, but there
seemed to be potential there. She asked what I was up to, so
I told her about my dance class. "What kind of dance?" she
asked me. I laughed, feeling kind of excited to share my new
discovery. I feigned mild embarrassment in order to soften the
edges, make it more socially acceptable.

"Actually, this is kind of embarrassing, but it's pole dance,"
I replied.

What crossed her eyes at first flickered as confusion
then morphed into withdrawal. The conversation was over
before it even started. She shifted uncomfortably in her
metal folding chair, murmured, "Ah," and looked back at the
boys playing basketball, casually dismissing me and my fake
embarrassment, and instead pretending to be interested in
seven-year-olds attempting to play basketball. My attempt to
discuss pole dancing with a fellow mom shut down, I felt a
flush of heat enter my face. What was I thinking? Of course,
that was her reaction. This was suburban Connecticut, for
goodness sake. People come here to get away from the type of
moms who pole dance.

I'd spent years in Connecticut trying to fit in, squeezing
myself into a "Connecticut housewife" and "good mom" costume that never really fit. I wanted to be the best mom I could

possibly be to my kids, but I also wanted to project the right image to others in my community.

The price I paid for pretending was steep. By abandoning myself in favor of a false image, I'd become depressed, anxious, overweight, and unhappy. It was time to take off the uncomfortable, ill-fitting costume and start being myself. But as a result of that decision, I'd pay a different price, one that was reflected in Karen's face.

But couldn't I still be a great mom, even if I didn't quite fit the mold of what the traditional good mom looked like in my town? I thought I could…but I wasn't sure if I could handle the idea that not everyone would be happy with the changes I was making for myself. That stuff is deeply ingrained in all of us.

As girls, we're taught from a young age to do our best to please others, even at the expense of our own needs. We're taught to be nice, to be attractive and skinny, to smile, to be quiet. We're told not to be bossy or difficult, not to get angry or cause trouble or be rebellious. We're taught that our value in the world hinges on our ability to please others. We're raised to avoid making other people uncomfortable in any way. We're raised to take on everything and never complain— or if we do, do it privately.

Katty Kay and Claire Shipman, in their book *The Confidence Code*, report that it's actually in our DNA as women to be pleasers and avoid conflict, because estrogen encourages bonding and connection. We're wired to want to be liked and to seek out the approval of others. Combine the hardwiring we're born with and the way we're brought up to be pleasers by our parents and society at large, and we create a situation where all our instincts tell us to be pleasing to others, even if it's at our own expense.

We want to avoid the uncomfortable feelings associated with disappointing others or confrontation, so we shove our own needs out the door and don't push back in difficult situations. We want to be liked, to avoid the crushing anxiety that comes when other people disapprove of us. And because this societal conditioning starts so early in life, we don't get to practice difficult conversations growing up, making them extraordinarily uncomfortable for us as adults.

The result of all that societal training is that we internalize the message that our needs, our opinions, our voices, and our desires *are less important* than those of other people. We become a mirror of what other people want, rather than who we really are. And the more we focus on what other people want, the more our own identities shrink in comparison. We suppress our authentic selves in favor of a more pleasing, more pliant version of ourselves. And all of a sudden, there are two versions of us. There's our real, authentic self, which gets hidden away, and then there's the "perfect" version of our self that we present to the world. We become disconnected from our authentic selves, we literally abandon ourselves, in order to be pleasing to others, to be accepted and loved.

And that abandonment explodes when we become mothers. When we have kids, we seamlessly transition from being a "good girl" to a "good mom." All the old scripts continue to apply, telling us to put everyone else's needs first and our own needs last. We try to please our kids, our partners, our parents, our in-laws, and our friends, depriving ourselves of fulfillment of our own needs. We long ago lost touch with our authentic selves, in favor of a version of ourselves that we perceive as more acceptable to our families and society as a whole.

After all of that, we find ourselves feeling empty, depleted, sad, and overwhelmed, and we can't figure out why. Rather than celebrating ourselves, we hide ourselves away, ashamed of who we really are because we think who we really are is not good enough or lovable. Humans are insecure about being not good enough, and this insecurity shows up in our quest to be the best moms we can be. We overcompensate in order to prove to everyone that we are, in fact, good moms.

There's a price to be paid for abandoning your authentic self: *abandoning yourself in order to please others is a recipe for misery and unhappiness.*

Good Mom Types

Many of us fall loosely into one or more of the good mom types.

The Martyr Mom

This mom type is very common. We might all embody a bit of the martyr mom. Unfortunately, she's become the gold standard for what a good mom looks like in our society today. Her defining feature is that she puts herself last, seemingly has no needs of her own, and as a result takes better care of her family than she does herself. She doesn't take time for herself because whenever she tries to, she feels guilty. She tells herself she doesn't have the time, money, or energy for herself, and she really believes it. There is, however, an interesting secondary benefit to being a martyr mom: the constant sacrifice seems to give us permission to feel superior on some levels.

The Pleaser Mom

The pleaser mom lives for praise from others. She wants to make everybody happy, from her kids to her partner to her friends and her extended family…as well as the staff at her kids' school, the entirety of the PTA, and even the guy who picks up her garbage. If anyone's not happy with her, it affects her mood and makes her unhappy. She needs others' approval like she needs oxygen. The problem is, she doesn't feel good about herself, and she gets all her validation externally. This sets up a vicious cycle where she's constantly abandoning herself in order to please others.

The Crazy Busy Mom

Whenever you run into this mom, she's like a swirling vortex of chaos. You ask her how she's doing, and the reply is, invariably, "Oh my god, I'm so crazy busy!" It's easy to recognize this mom because you'll feel utterly exhausted just listening to her. She might be a working mom, or she might be an at-home mom. She fills her day with activity, and her kids are overscheduled with extracurriculars and sports each day until bedtime. It's like if she can just do enough, put in enough hours, and crush every goal on her to-do list, she'll be a good mom. The danger with this mom type is what's lurking beneath. Why does she need to be busy all the time? When she's not busy, she feels a crushing sense of anxiety that she's not doing enough.

The Perfect Mom

She's the president of the PTA and manages her monthly meetings every bit as efficiently as she managed her staff during her pre-kid Wall Street days. Her home is impeccable, from the white picket fence to the high-end stainless-steel appliances right down to the perfectly matched tassels on her window treatments. She always seems to have it together, with her perfectly put together outfit and her perfectly behaved kids and her perfectly spotless luxury SUV. Here's the truth about the perfect mom—she's just as messed up and unsure of herself as all the rest of us. But by making you think she has it all together, she feels better about herself.

The Helicopter Mom

She checks her kids' social media feeds, she checks their homework…sometimes, she actually does their homework. This is the mom who actually fills out the college applications because her kid is too busy. She can't stand for her kids to fail in any area of life so she takes over to ensure success. The helicopter mom can also sometimes be known as a control freak. Deep down, she's convinced that her kids' achievements are her achievements—and if her kids don't excel, she's not doing a good enough job as a mom.

The Sanctimommy

This opinionated mom will tell you exactly what she thinks of your parenting choices, and she's 100 percent certain that she is correct. She has no tolerance for kids who are unruly, a home that's untidy, or meals that are not home-cooked and organic…and she'll be happy to share her opinions on how you can make better choices. From what shows you should let your child watch (if any!) to what you should pack for lunch or prepare for dinner to how many hours of sleep your child should be getting, this mom is nothing if not absolutely certain she's doing it right. Her sanctimoniousness comes from, once again, a need to do parenting "right." It may feel like she's looking down on you for your choices, but deep down, she's afraid she's not good enough.

Do you recognize yourself in any of these types?

You probably have elements of more than one of these moms in your personality. We all do. I've had moments of martyr mom syndrome that I've had to overcome, with large doses of pleaser mom as well.

What do all the mom types have in common?

These are all moms who proudly wear the label of *The Good Mom*, who seem to have it all together, but under the surface are in serious need of self-care. They routinely deprive themselves, giving all their resources—their love, time, energy, heart, and soul—to their kids. Martyr mom quietly sacrifices herself for her kids. Pleaser mom loses herself trying to make everyone else happy. Perfect mom is depriving herself of pleasure and joy in her drive to achieve. Helicopter mom is terrified of losing control over her kids' lives. And sanctimommy is trying to make herself feel more secure in an uncertain world.

The result of all this deprivation is that all these moms are *starving*. They've bought into the idea that good moms put themselves last. To use a food analogy, let's say there's a huge banquet table filled with the most delicious foods. The good mom lets everyone else fill their plates, and by the time she gets to the table, there's nothing left. In this analogy, and in life, the good mom needs to realize that it's okay to feed herself too. That feeding herself, that sharing in the abundant bounty from the banquet table of life, doesn't make her any less of a good mom.

She may argue with me on that point. Her greatest fear is that if she lives life on her terms, if she puts her needs on the same level as the needs of her partner and kids, she'll be neglecting or depriving her kids of something important, something they can't go without. She won't be a good mom. This is the cultural conditioning talking, not rational thinking.

Our kids want our happiness. We, as moms, are the center of their world, the sun that shines down on them each day and gives them the strength to go out into the world. We are the earth mothers who provide grounding and stability to our kids. Our warmth and positive energy, our authentic happiness, are a source of strength and courage for them. In order to share it with our kids, we have to start by giving it to ourselves.

Decide to Meet Your Needs

A crucial step in overcoming the mom-life crisis is being completely done with the good mom myth and the notion that the only way to be a good mom, in the current cultural definition, is to toss aside your own needs. No. We're done with the unreasonable expectations, we're done with the perfectionistic standards, we're done with self-sacrifice, we're done with taking care of everyone else with no thought for ourselves. We're done with guilt, overwhelm, and self-recrimination.

We're done.

Do you want to be the best, most authentic version of yourself?

Do you want to be as healthy and happy as you can be?

Do you want to take care of yourself as well as you take care of your kids?

Then you've made the decision.

Stop trying to live up to the myth of the good mom, and you're ready to overcome your own mom-life crisis.

Clear the path toward authentic self-care by making the decision to let go of the myth of the good mom. Realize that the myth of the good mom is just that—a myth. It's a myth that by simply giving and giving of yourself, that by depriving yourself, pleasing others, following the rules, and keeping yourself small, you'll be a better or happier mom. It's a myth that by pleasing others or sacrificing yourself to be a good mom, you'll finally be "good enough."

The truth is, you're already good enough. There's nothing you need to prove, to anyone, in order to be worthy of love.

How to Decide

If you have a hard time understanding why this *deciding* is important, let's put it in terms most of us understand. Have you ever tried to lose weight? Likely, yes. We all have. Here are a couple of scenarios that may occur:

1. You want to lose ten pounds. And you think about it every day. Randomly, you reduce your food intake all day. By dinner, you are starving, so you eat a huge meal. And then you beat yourself up and vow to do better tomorrow.

2. You want to lose ten pounds. So you decide to put a plan in place. You start keeping a food diary and you write down every bite you put in your mouth. You get rid of all the processed foods in your pantry so you won't be tempted. You go to the farmers' market and stock up on your favorite fresh fruits and vegetables. You put together a meal plan for the week and do the prep work on Sunday so that you'll be prepared for the rest of the week.

Which one of these weight-loss scenarios is more likely to succeed?

Number two. Why? Because you made a decision and made a plan to back it up.

It's just as important to decide *this is what you want* and then to create a plan when it comes to self-care. *I want to be the best possible version of myself, the happiest and healthiest I can possibly be, and I'm willing to do what it takes to get there.*

Making the decision is critical because without it, you won't feel the motivation to make important changes in your life. Inertia is a powerful force—it's a lot easier to fall back on our old patterns than it is to make meaningful changes. We all want to avoid pain. It's human nature. And while self-care isn't painful, changing our lives is something many of us resist because we're afraid, and fear can be emotionally painful. So we avoid it. We continue with the status quo, sticking with our metaphorical "comfort food" of old patterns and behaviors, because it's what we know.

Self-care, in whatever form it takes for you, will make you a better, happier, more fulfilled mom. When we start to love ourselves, meet our own needs, and take care of ourselves, we actually have more love, more time, and more energy to give our families, because we're giving from a place of fullness and abundance.

Just like many of us eventually come to love, and even crave, working out and eating healthy foods, you'll begin to crave self-care. Once you decide to incorporate it into your life, you'll wonder how you lived without it for so long.

You don't have to start pole dancing, though I highly recommend it, but find something that feeds you. And when you find it, don't be afraid of it. By feeding yourself, you're creating a fuller container from which to love and care for not just yourself, but also for everyone else in your life.

Today's To-Dos: Bust the Good Mom Myth

They key to busting the myth is in knowing that you deserve it, and that everyone in your life is going to benefit from it. The steps you take in this book will help you start feeding yourself a healthy, consistent diet of love and care and end the legacy of deprivation.

Be specific and detailed in answering the following questions:

1. In what ways have you sacrificed yourself in order to meet the cultural standard of a good mom?

Some ideas to get you started: Maybe you've given up your creative outlets, your physical fitness or healthy eating habits, your childhood friendships, your passion for cooking or dance or opera, or alone time for yourself.

2. What have you given up that you really miss? Are there any activities you could get lost in, that made you lose track of time for hours? To answer this, close your eyes and consider the activities that really lit you up as a kid and then as an adult, before having kids.

3. What parts of you have you hidden or suppressed in order to meet the cultural standard of a good mom?

Chapter 4

THE SIX PILLARS OF SELF-CARE

Love yourself first and everything else falls into line. You really have to love yourself to get anything done in this world.

—*LUCILLE BALL*

"Mom has PMS. Again," I overheard Jenna say.

I couldn't see her, but I could picture the exact look on her ten-year-old face, eye roll included. I stood at the stove in the kitchen, making a big pot of chili for the kids for dinner, as homemade cornbread cooked in the oven. There was a tiny hallway off the kitchen, near where I stood, that led to the playroom where the kids were talking. They clearly didn't know I was listening.

"Mom *always* has PMS," Andrew replied, his voice filled with sass. At twelve, he spoke with the authority of the oldest child and, therefore, the expert on all mom-related things.

"The week before, the week during, and the week after her period. Three weeks per month, basically," he concluded. The two of them cracked up at the apparent truth of Andrew's statement, that I was cranky and irritable *almost all the time.* I gave the food in the pot on the stove a little stir and felt my eyes well up with tears. *Here we go again.* Andrew was right—even when it wasn't that time of the month, I was moody and irritable most of the time, with a hair-trigger temper and tears that came far more easily than they used to. It was heartbreaking to learn that the kids were so aware, that my moods actually impacted them.

I wiped my eyes and kept stirring. *Stop feeling sorry for yourself.* I didn't want to be cranky and PMS-y all the time. A few months into attending classes at the pole dance studio, I loved it. But I realized that just taking a dance class once a week wasn't enough to change my overall mood. It helped day-to-day, but I needed more. I needed to make more systemic changes.

Seated on Sherry's immaculate gray couch a few days later, I relayed the conversation I'd overheard between my two oldest kids. I secretly hoped Sherry and I would laugh it off and move on to discuss something simpler, but instead she simply looked at me with concern.

Finally, she spoke.

"That's quite a wake-up call, isn't it," she said.

Ugh. I sat with my head in my hands. I knew in my heart I couldn't keep living my life the way I'd been living it. All I'd ever wanted was to be a good mom, and here I was, facing the cold reality. I wasn't happy, and it was obvious to everyone, including my kids. I had to believe my unhappiness was impacting my parenting. Not only that, but I was inadvertently teaching the kids the wrong lessons about being a mom.

Sherry and I had been talking for months about the concept of self-care, but so far it was only an intellectual exercise for me. I hadn't put any of her suggestions into practice yet. I'd learned from Sherry that self-care involved a lot more than just adding a little bit of me-time each week, that the changes required went deeper and had much more impact. It was challenging to let go of my old ways after so many years. But I needed a new approach, and I had a really good reason to do it. It wasn't for me anymore…it was for my kids.

Playing the Long Game with Self-Care

There have been countless books and articles written about self-care for moms, and almost all of them emphasize the importance of taking time each week for you. Get a mani-pedi! Go for a walk with your best friend! Read a book! Go on date night with your partner! I'm not saying these aren't great suggestions—all are fun things to do.

But they're tactical, not strategic. And they're not enough on their own to effect change. Believe me when I say that getting your nails done for half an hour, while pleasurable in the moment, is not going to help with your overall wellness and happiness on a long-term basis. That would be like going to the gym once and thinking the result will be great health and fitness for life.

Putting yourself on the to-do list, therefore, requires a broad, all-encompassing system. The approach that's most effective is multipronged and addresses the issue at the deepest level.

What Is Self-care?

Self-care is knowing you matter and making choices every day that ensure you're at your physical, mental, emotional, and spiritual best. It's deciding that you're fully responsible for your life, your choices, and your well-being. It's a mindset shift based on the idea that your happiness and your fulfillment are important. It's saying, *I count. I matter. My voice and my needs matter.* It requires respect and love for yourself. It requires the discipline to say yes to things that benefit you and no to things that don't, even though those things may feel good in the moment.

It's not immediate gratification. It's about the bigger picture of who you are and who you want to be as a woman. It's about loving yourself enough to do what's best for you, today and in the future. It's about having the discipline to practice it consciously every day.

It's saying no to that second (or third) margarita at dinner because you want to feel your best tomorrow. It's committing to an exercise program or a meditation practice because you know how great it makes you feel. It's putting on sunscreen, getting a mammogram, eating your broccoli. It's choosing not to engage with toxic people. It's turning off the television and going to sleep. It's seeing a therapist when life's challenges feel overwhelming.

Self-care is self-love. It's loving yourself as much as you love your kids and *devoting as much thought, time, and energy to your own needs as you devote to your kids' happiness and well-being.*

Identifying our needs can be tricky, because we've been out of touch with them for so long. Or we've become so accustomed to not having our needs met that we've lowered our expectations drastically. We think, falsely, that if we expect our needs won't be met, we won't be disappointed when, inevitably, we're correct. Or, worst of all, we think we're "bad" for having needs. What kind of a mom thinks of herself, we wonder? This thinking is a sickness among moms today. We actually beat ourselves up for needing sleep or alone time.

Needs are also hard to acknowledge because we see satisfying them as a way of taking from our children. We don't realize that *having our needs met* is a good thing for our kids.

Exercising self-care starts with paying attention to your basic needs, those fundamentals that ensure you're at your best, ready to take on whatever life throws at you.

The Fundamentals

Assuming you've already got a roof over your head, food in your fridge, and a warm bed to sleep in each night, then it's time to focus on basic fundamentals often ignored by moms. These are the foundation of self-care, without which any additional self-care practices won't be as effective. Think of it like building a house. You wouldn't build a house without a solid foundation, would you? By building your self-care practice on a solid foundation of fundamentals, you're ensuring your own success.

Pillar #1: Sleep

We all know how terrible it feels when we don't get enough sleep. We get cranky and irritable, we have trouble concentrating during the day, and we lack our usual amount of energy. Multiple studies provide scientific evidence for what we already know, that sleep is vital for our physical and mental wellness.

According to the Division of Sleep Medicine at Harvard Medical School, the short- and long-term consequences of lack of sleep are significant:

In the short term, a lack of adequate sleep can affect judgment, mood, ability to learn and retain information, and may increase the risk of serious accidents and injury. In the long term, chronic sleep deprivation may lead to a host of health problems including obesity, diabetes, cardiovascular disease, and even early mortality.

My informal polling suggests that for many of us moms, we stopped sleeping when our kids were babies and we never really started again. As important as we all know sleep is to our health, it's one of those priorities that gets pushed to the bottom of the list and seems to stay there indefinitely.

There's a reality when our kids are babies and toddlers that, unless our kids are that rare breed that sleep through the night from an early age, we're going to be sleep deprived for a few months or even years. My friend Lori has a three-year-old who still wakes her up every two hours. If you're still in the thick of it, please know this is not forever! It's temporary, and eventually you'll sleep again.

Once those days mercifully come to an end, begin to prioritize sleep. You need to feel your best every day. And that can only happen if you've slept.

I know it's tempting to stay up late watching another episode of your favorite Netflix show, reading the latest bestseller, or watching late-night comedy shows. I have total FOMO nearly every night when I go to sleep. If you're worried about missing something or not getting that extra work in, or whatever it is you think you need to do after the kids have gone to sleep—consider, bigger picture, what you really want. Do you want to be your best, happiest, healthiest self tomorrow? Then turn off the light!

Okay, fair enough, sometimes turning the light off isn't enough. Try these tips:

✧ *Build a bedtime routine.* Your routine may include things like a bath, a book, chamomile tea, and time to connect with your partner. Let it be relaxing, soothing, and calming. It should also include a consistent lights-out time each night.

✧ *Remove your phone from your bedroom,* or at least move it out of reach, and turn off the ringer and notifications to minimize distractions.

✧ *Reduce your exposure to blue light at least two hours before bedtime.* Blue light, which comes from phones, tablets, and computers, tricks your circadian rhythm by making your body think it's daytime.

✧ *Transform your bedroom into a soothing, relaxing sanctuary.* I recommend getting the softest, coziest, highest-quality sheets, blankets, and pillows your budget will allow. Find the optimum room temperature for you. Use soft light bulbs in bedside lamps, rather than harsh overhead lighting.

✧ *Share the nighttime responsibilities* if you have a partner and you still have young kids. For example, you can divide the evening into shifts, and you'll offer to handle the first shift. That way you can get a long block of sleep from midnight to 6:00 a.m.

✧ If you struggle with insomnia, many people have had success with *melatonin, valerian root, magnesium, lavender oil, or (my personal favorite) CBD oil.* Try these supplements one at a time (check with your doctor first) to see which one works for you.

Pillar #2: Food and Drink

"I deserve it!"

"Just one more!"

"I need a treat today!"

How many times have you heard yourself saying this, or something like it, as you reached for that warm, heaping plate of nachos swimming in melted cheese? Or the fresh-from-the-oven chocolate chip cookies that make your kitchen smell like the local bakery? Or the full-bodied red wine that seems to go down easier with each glass? It's an evil cycle: eat to feel better and then feel self-loathing for eating (or drinking) too much.

Instead of numbing with food and wine, eat healthfully. Doing so is one fundamental step toward self-care because it speaks directly to your physical, emotional, and mental health, not just today but in the long term. Your food and drink choices impact your weight, how you feel, your mood, how you sleep, and your health. Do you want more energy? To maintain your weight? To lose weight?

Try these tips:

⬥ Do your research. There are so many eating plans that work, whether you want to adjust your weight or just improve your health. Self-care is about deciding what you want and finding the eating plan that works best for you.

⬥ Love yourself. Don't get crazy. *Eating healthy isn't about getting skinny.* It's about loving and cherishing your beautiful self enough to put nourishing fuel in your body. That means making healthy choices that are right for you, while also accepting yourself as you are right now. No beating yourself up or being hard on yourself is allowed. Ever.

✧ The same principles apply to drinking alcohol. Self-care, for me, means having one or two drinks and that's it. I've learned that, for my body, two drinks is my limit if I want to feel good, get a good night's sleep, and be productive the next day. You need to figure out yours. Find your cutoff and stick to it.

Pillar #3: Exercise

"I'd love to exercise more, if I only had more time."

Who else has said that to themselves? I have certainly fallen into that trap. Everyone knows the benefits of exercise: it helps stabilize your mood, it gives you energy, it helps you sleep better, it's good for your muscles and bones. I could go on and on. But still, exercise was at the bottom of my to-do list for years, always the first thing to go when the demands of raising kids and working got to be too much.

I'd wake up every day motivated, with the best intentions to squeeze in a workout, but then life would happen, the day would get away from me, and I'd end up going weeks without a good sweat. I didn't know how other moms did it—how were they able to juggle everything in life and also get in a workout every day, or even just a few times a week?

Exercise is one of the things that makes us happy. Like, really happy. It floods our brain with feel-good chemicals. So when you're not exercising, you're not positioning yourself to be as happy and healthy as you can possibly be. I don't exercise for weight management. I do it because it ensures my mood will be stable and positive for the day.

You don't need to sweat profusely or achieve six-pack abs in order to have an effective exercise program. For me, the only criteria for a good workout is that it gets me off the couch and makes me feel strong, energetic, and happy for the rest of the day. Sometimes it's a sweaty spin or boxing class, sometimes it's a delicious dance class, and sometimes it's a leisurely walk with a friend. It all counts!

Try these tips:

✧ Schedule your workouts in your calendar at the beginning of each week. This is a way of saying, *Exercise is a priority for me and I'm making time for it.* Write it down each day in pen, like any other appointment. Block out the time. When you schedule your workouts, you create a routine for yourself, and eventually working out can become just as much a part of your daily routine as brushing your teeth. I've come to crave my workout as much as I crave my morning coffee (well, almost as much).

✧ Find workouts you enjoy, so you'll be more likely to do them.

✧ Workouts don't have to be strenuous to be effective. As long as your body's moving, it counts.

Pillar #4: Daily Chill Time

One late afternoon during my mom-life crisis, I decided to try meditation. I'd been reading about it for months and was intrigued about the potential benefits, like relief from stress and anxiety, that came from practicing for only ten minutes per day. It seemed perfect for my time-starved lifestyle.

I put a Disney DVD on for the kids, fed them a snack, and explained I was going up to my room for ten minutes of alone time. Finding them agreeable, I went upstairs, locked the bedroom door, and sat on the little meditation cushion I'd purchased at Whole Foods for this occasion.

The technique from my meditation instruction book called for simply focusing on the breath, the inhale and exhale. I sat on my cushion, closed my eyes, and started to slow my breathing. *Inhale. Exhale.* I was just starting to sense a steady, calm feeling in my body when I started to hear sounds outside my bedroom door, whispering, giggling, and shuffling footsteps.

I noticed the sounds then brought my attention back to my breath, just as the book taught me. Then the sounds started to get louder. I became aware that the kids were jostling the doorknob, pushing it back and forth, trying to get the door open.

"Ten minutes, guys!" I said, loud enough so they could hear. My breathing got shallower, and it felt like my heart rate was going up. This was not helping me get more zen.

It got quiet again. *Inhale, exhale.* My heart rate slowed again as I recentered myself and focused on my breathing.

That's when I heard the sounds of bare feet running up the hall. It sounded as though they'd started at the other end of the hallway and were heading toward my room. I shook my head and braced myself as I sensed what was to come. *Oh no. Don't do it.* Then I heard the massive THUD of a body against my bedroom door that shook the whole room, followed by a CRASH against the floor.

I opened my eyes, blinked. *My children were literally hurling their bodies against my door, trying to break it down.*

I blew out the candle, got off my pillow, and stormed out of the room. Livid, I lost my temper. "All I wanted was ten minutes, and your reaction is to try to break my door down? Not okay!"

I learned my lesson. After that incident, I started waking up early to meditate, before the kids were up, and that worked out much better for everyone.

Stress management, or what I like to call *daily chill time,* is every bit as important as the other items in this chapter. Stress is unavoidable in life, and it can cause all sorts of health issues and emotional issues. So it's critical to find methods of managing it that work for you.

Daily chill time is a way to take ten minutes each day to recharge. Just ten minutes. You don't have to meditate to do it either. The list below offers up many ideas to try, or you may have some of your own. What's important is that you mindfully choose activities that actually help you recharge. You should emerge from your daily chill time feeling calm, centered, and ready to take on the challenges of the day.

What Is a Mindful Recharge?

Any activity that is tailored to your unique personality and needs, and that is given your 100 percent undistracted attention. For example, if you're an extrovert, talking on the phone with a close friend for ten minutes may help you recharge. But if you're an introvert (like me), ten minutes of talking may be exhausting. In that case, you'd be better off doing something completely alone.

My friend Kathleen practices yoga by herself every morning before her kids wake up, because it quiets her racing mind and helps her feel centered and connected to her heart and soul. She only does a few poses, just enough to get her blood flowing and her mind calm, so it takes less than fifteen minutes.

My friend Lisa puts on slow, sexy music and moves her body. Her movements are similar to the warm-up from her pole dance class, where she stretches and slithers and rolls and undulates her body. She only dances to two or three songs before she feels full, and then she begins the rest of her morning routine. This brief interlude allows her to feel deliciously connected to her body and her femininity all day.

And then there's Laura, who takes at least ten minutes each afternoon to dive into whatever book she's reading. Reading calms her body and mind and helps her relax before the dinner-bath-bed routine.

Here are a few examples of daily chill time activities:

Call a friend

Listen to music (making playlists is one of my favorite chill-time activities!)

Say affirmations

Meditate

Practice yoga

Walk

Dance

Write in your journal

Make a gratitude list

Practice deep-breathing exercises

Nap

Not sure how to achieve daily chill time? Try these tips:

✧ Try to schedule your daily chill time for a time when the kids are busy doing other things, like sleeping or going to school.

- ✧ Make a plan. Decide in advance when you're going to take your daily chill time and schedule it in your calendar.

- ✧ Be consistent. Daily chill time only takes ten minutes, so try to squeeze it in every day if possible.

- ✧ Make it a goal to move through life with as little tension in your body as possible. We spend so much time clenched, whether in our jaws, our fists, our legs. Use your daily chill time to remind yourself to unclench and relax your entire body.

Pillar #5: Love and Connection

The need for connection and community is primal,
as fundamental as the need for air, water, and food.

—Dr. Dean Ornish

Studies have shown that the people who are the happiest as they age are those with deep, meaningful connections with others. It's the quality of these relationships that matters, not the quantity. Close social connections are as important for your health as, if not more important than, your weight and level of exercise. People are far more likely to get sick, depressed, or anxious if they're lonely or isolated. Connection with others actually strengthens our immune systems. A strong sense of connection and community is an important step toward protecting your health and well-being and living a longer life.

It's also a way to make your life better and more enjoyable. Social connections strengthen our sense of self-esteem and make us more empathetic and more cooperative. So, the stronger our social connections, the healthier we are, and the better we feel. And when we're feeling healthy and feeling strong emotionally, we're more likely to engage more in deep connections with others. This creates an ongoing loop in which we realize ongoing health and wellness benefits.

This might sound strange to someone without kids, but it can be lonely and isolating to be a mom. It seems that in our modern culture, we no longer have the *it takes a village* mentality toward raising kids. Many of us isolate ourselves, thinking we have to go it alone, and sometimes find it more difficult to make friends as we age. We don't have as much social time as we did in high school and college, and once we have kids, we don't always prioritize friendships in the same way we once did.

I have made social interaction a pillar of self-care because it is often relegated to the bottom of the list because it's considered a luxury, something we can focus on later, as time permits.

During my mom-life crisis, I didn't make time for friends. It was all kids, all the time. This posed a problem when a friend wanted to throw me a fortieth birthday party. I literally didn't know who to invite. I had a lot of "friends" but few *real* friends. And it was my own fault…I hadn't put in the effort because I had put all my energy toward raising my kids (that's the martyr mom in action!).

For some people, friends come easily and naturally, but for the rest of us, it takes more effort. As an introvert, I could easily stay inside all the time and have little contact with the outside world, other than through social media. It's work for me to put myself out there and make friends and nurture those friendships. But over time, I have done it because it's a basic human need.

You may be thinking, *But I have my husband/spouse/ life partner!* Studies have shown that marriages are actually healthier when you avoid putting your spouse into the role of being everything to you. When you expect your spouse to be not only your life partner and lover but also your only best friend and sounding board, that puts a lot of pressure on your marriage.

Real friends, outside of your marriage, give you a different perspective. They give you a sense of community. They give you someone to talk to when your spouse is driving you crazy. They give you fresh ideas when your kid is driving you crazy. Friends remind you that you're not just a mom—you're an adult woman with a life that happened before kids and that will continue to happen after the kids leave your house to embark on their own lives.

Try these tips:

✧ Seek out like-minded people. If you don't have a couple of good friends, look into groups in your area that are based around common interests. My friend Lesley made lots of good friends through her church, while my friend Laura made nearly all her friends through a local running club.

✧ Prioritize friendships. Don't underestimate the importance of friends to your emotional health and happiness. I still don't have a huge group of friends…but now, years after my mom-life crisis, I have four or five women I could call at any hour of the night and I know they'd be there for me.

✧ Make a few good, strong friendships, not twenty casual ones. You can have as many book clubs or cocktail parties as you want, but take the time to make the effort to really connect with and stay in touch with a few women you can call at any hour of the night, women you can talk to about anything.

Pillar #6: Kindness

> *Kindness to yourself is one of the most important elements of self-care.*
>
> —*TERRY DEMEO*

One of the most important and fundamental aspects of self-care, an area that is absolutely crucial, is kindness. *To yourself.* As moms, we beat ourselves up for everything, and that has got to change. We make ourselves miserable with our negative self-talk that never ever shuts up. We're hard on ourselves for what we think, what we feel, what we say, what we do, what we don't do, you name it. We're professional criticizers, and our favorite target is ourselves. The antidote is to be kind and to treat ourselves with compassion.

Think of the way you talk to yourself when you mess up or make a mistake. Are you unduly hard on yourself? You may not think you're hard on yourself, but ask yourself, do you talk the same way to people you love, such as your best friend or your daughter? Do you bring up past mistakes with your best friend? Do you tell her she's a shitty mom or that her kids are going to hate her because of her poor decisions? No. You're nicer to other people than you are to you, I suspect.

"But I deserve it sometimes!" you may protest. I disagree. There's no upside to beating yourself up. It doesn't make you a better mom. It doesn't make you try harder next time. If you think you messed up somehow, the most productive way to handle it is to notice, decide you'll do better next time, make any changes that need to be made in order to make that happen, and then *let it go.* Don't ruminate, don't endlessly replay it, don't tell yourself it means something about who you are as a mom.

Your thoughts can take off like a runaway train that brings you, the poor unsuspecting passenger, along for the ride. Sometimes that train can take you to dark places, at warp speed, and you feel powerless to stop it. Fortunately, there are tools at our disposal that allow us to get off that train before it leaves the station, mostly by noticing our thoughts and letting them go, rather than attaching to them and believing them to be the gospel truth.

We like to think we have control in life, but in truth, we don't have control over most things. *One of the few things in life we actually* do *have control over is how we handle what happens.* We can choose to be nice to ourselves no matter what our external circumstances are.

Good relationships are all about treating each other with kindness and respect, and a good relationship with yourself starts with treating yourself with kindness and respect too. It's time to start including yourself on your list of people whom you treat with kindness and respect.

Rewrite the Story

The first step toward being kind to yourself is to notice that the negative thoughts you're having are nothing more than a story you're choosing to tell yourself. And, miraculously, you have the ability to choose to tell yourself a different story...a story that's just as true. For example, I have told myself, "I'm a shitty mom, and I'm failing miserably at raising my children." I not only told myself this story, I bought into it, internalized it, and let it eat away at me from the inside. It made me feel terrible, it made me lose sleep, and it put me in a worse mood than I already was in.

Here's an alternative story I could have told myself, had I chosen to be kind to myself all those years ago: "I'm doing my best, but I'm overwhelmed and overbooked, and it's making me less than my best self. I'm going to take a look at my priorities and make adjustments so that I start feeling happier." This story is *just as true* as the first one, but it's kinder, more compassionate, and, ultimately, more productive. This story would have inspired me to make changes, rather than inspiring me to do nothing except feel sorry for myself for so long.

Reshaping your story is freedom from torturing yourself with needless self-flagellation and instead basking in your own brilliance. You're amazing. You're doing your best. Your kids feel loved and cherished. You can choose to see yourself through a negative lens, if you want…or you can choose to change your perception. See yourself through the eyes of your mom, your best friend, or some other benevolent creature. You deserve to be given the benefit of the doubt, even when you royally mess up, because you're awesome and you're doing your best. Shift your reality to a more positive story and see how your whole life starts to shift.

Part of rewriting the story is letting go of some bad old thoughts. Try to ground yourself in the present moment, letting go of past and future. Then try to see yourself not as your thoughts, but as an objective observer of your thoughts. Recognize that your negative thoughts are not you. Your thoughts are like clouds, temporarily passing by as they cross a beautiful blue sky. You are the person observing those thoughts, and you can choose to let them pass, just like clouds.

Once you've let your thoughts go gently into the ether, remind yourself of what's true. It might help to write these truths down or make a note on your phone. You're a great mom, you're doing an amazing job, you love your kids and they love you. You do your best every day with the skills and resources you currently have available to you. You're not perfect, nor are you intended to be. You're a human and you make mistakes sometimes just like everybody else. You say and do stupid things sometimes—we all do. You're still worthy of kindness and respect from yourself (and everyone else).

Self-Love and Self-Care Are Not Selfish

It can be a challenge for us as moms to think of ourselves, to carve out and take up space for ourselves, to say that we matter. But what I learned from Sherry is that nothing is more important than doing so, if I want to feel my best and live my best life every day and be the kind of mom and person I want to be.

It's not selfish. Self-care makes you the best possible version of yourself, a person who makes the choices that ensure she's at the top of her game, every single day.

It also takes discipline to live this way. It's so easy and can be really fun to stay up late, drink too much, skip the workout. It's easy to fall into a rut of negative self-talk. It takes work and effort to practice self-care day in and day out, to make choices that may not be the easiest but are the ones that are going to benefit you and make you feel your best.

I don't want to be the mom who's cranky three out of four weeks per month. I don't want to be the mom who's not feeling or looking her best. I want to be there for my kids in the best way I can be. I want to be my best self, every day. The only way to do that is to practice self-care each and every day.

Today's To-Dos: Self-Care

Make an action plan by answering the following questions in your journal.

How many hours of sleep per night, on average, are you getting? How many hours would you like to get?

Are you happy with your current eating plan? Why or why not? What changes do you need to make to reach a point where you feel great?

Are you happy with your current fitness level? Why or why not? What changes do you need to make to feel great about your fitness?

Are you taking time each day just for you?

Are you engaged with your partner, your family, and your friends? Are you happy with your current friendships and level of engagement?

Are you kind to yourself? Use your journal to start tracking the thoughts you have and the things you say to yourself. Question those thoughts by asking yourself if the thought is really true.*

*For more in-depth guidance on the practice of questioning your thoughts, read Byron Katie's excellent book, *Loving What Is.*

Chapter 5
TAMING THE GUILT MONSTER

*There's no way to be a perfect mother and
a million ways to be a good one.*

—JILL CHURCHILL

When I first started my company, I set up an office in town (about half a mile from home, and across the street from the kids' school) so I could work while my older kids were in school and be either home or at school at a moment's notice, if necessary.

I worked during the school day, leaving at 3:00 p.m. to pick up Andrew and Jenna and go home. But the strangest thing happened. While at the office, I felt guilty about being at work and leaving my sweet little babies, Matt and Jamie, at home with our nanny. But then later, when I got home, I'd think about work and all the unfinished things I left there, and then I'd feel guilty that I wasn't working.

It seemed I always guilted myself into needing to be in the *other* place.

And while I'm aware that my situation was inherently privileged and not all moms are fortunate enough to have the choice as to whether or not to work, guilt is equal opportunity. It impacts those of us who work because we want to, those of us who work because circumstances deem it necessary, and those who do other things outside the home, such as take care of aging parents or volunteer work. It also impacts those of us who choose to stay home with our kids.

Guilt is a fact of life when you become a mom, no matter what choices you make. Because we care so deeply about our kids, we feel like anything less than what we deem as total perfection in the child-rearing department makes us deserving of our own harsh judgement. And how do we define perfection? Usually based on some impossible-to-attain ideal from an external source (I'm looking at you, Instagram) that has no bearing on the reality of life for most moms.

I can't tell you how many times I felt guilty and beat myself up because life wasn't perfectly perfect when the kids were little. I wasn't a perfectly happy, fulfilled mom, always smiling and happy and cooking organic meals in my immaculately clean kitchen. My kids weren't perfectly dressed or perfectly behaved. My home certainly wasn't perfectly decorated or organized. I saw depictions on TV of moms who never forgot to pack their kid's lunch for school, who never got frustrated sitting in traffic, who never sent their kid to school in a mismatched outfit, and I wondered, who are these people? And if they can keep it together, why can't I? I thought I was the one struggling, and everyone else had the secret to being a great, together mom. The guilt was crushing and constant.

Here's the thing about guilt: it's not helpful, and it's serving no purpose other than to shame and belittle you and make you feel bad about yourself.

Some people think feeling guilty will motivate them to do better or be better, but that's not the case. Guilt doesn't inspire you. It's all negative energy. Guilt is demoralizing and, as a result, demotivating.

Guilt is a sneaky form of perfectionism. I say sneaky because, unlike other forms of perfectionism, guilt doesn't rear its ugly head in an overt way. Instead, it sneaks in under the radar when you think you're minding your own business, going about your day. It starts quietly harassing you, telling you that your kids aren't going to thrive unless you breastfeed them exclusively for a full twelve months, or that your decision to go back to work is doing irreparable harm, or that taking time to go to the gym is selfish.

Guilt lies to us about our decisions, and it punishes us when we aren't doing anything wrong.

If there's only one thing you take away from this chapter, let it be this: *guilt is a liar and a bully.* And the only way to fight back against a bullying liar is with truth and objectivity.

Ultimately, it's important to let go of guilt, because it can drive you to make externally based choices that don't reflect your truth.

The Mom Reality

The objective reality of life for most moms is that our child-bearing years coincide with our career-building years. Most households in this country need two incomes. Most workdays don't end before school lets out. Most people can't take an unexpected day off when their child is sick or there's a snow day. Most women can't breastfeed exclusively and work outside the home. Maybe the problem is not with us, but with a society that's created a work environment that's so inhospitable to moms and a draconian parenting culture that demands nothing less than perfection.

The objective truth is we're all doing our best, for the most part, and *our best is good enough*. As much as we may want to create a Pinterest board–worthy home and family life, it's not reality and it's not attainable.

Many of us who were raised in the '70s and '80s remember the days of coming home to an empty house after school each day and watching TV all afternoon, eating Velveeta cheese, Twinkies, and TV dinners. We rode our bikes without helmets and wandered our neighborhoods till dark, our parents having no idea where we were or whom we were with.

Did our moms feel guilty? Not at all. Parenting wasn't a competitive sport back then, and there certainly wasn't the same amount of pressure to do it perfectly.

I'm not suggesting we go back to the hands-off, carefree parenting style that was popular in the '70s, before the idea of "parenting styles" even existed. I'm suggesting we've gone too far in the opposite direction and it's wreaking havoc on our psyches. Maybe it's time for the pendulum to swing back to the center, to a happy medium where we can be hands-on, involved moms, but not be so hard on ourselves when the realities of life lead us to make choices that aren't totally child-centric.

We can be working moms—or moms who have lives outside of our home and our kids—and still be hands-on, involved, and totally present in our kids' lives. We can have messy homes and still have happy, healthy kids. We can feed our kids food that isn't organic and stop breastfeeding when it's the right time for us, and they're still going to grow and thrive. It's all about the story we tell ourselves—it's about ditching guilt and treating ourselves with compassion. Our kids will be better off when we start treating ourselves with compassion, because when we're kind to ourselves, we're also kinder to everyone else.

How to Let Go of Guilt

Letting go of guilt isn't easy, but with practice, it can be done. Here are a few critical steps that will help.

Step 1: Know Your "Why"

A few years ago, I signed up to run in a half-marathon. My training schedule called for long runs on the weekends, sometimes taking me away from the house for up to two hours at a time. I felt so guilty about leaving the kids for that long. But, as anyone who's ever been a runner already knows, I felt amazing after my runs, energized, upbeat, and ready for my day. I became a better mom when I was training for the half-marathon, and everyone in my family benefited.

When you're engaged in an activity that makes you feel guilty, remind yourself *why* you're doing what you're doing. Whether you're working, socializing, exercising, or just sitting in bed binge-watching a Netflix show, know you're doing it because *it's what you need in this moment to be happy, and your being happy matters.*

Step 2: Know the Guilt Is Counterproductive

Think of something you feel guilty about with regard to your kids. Maybe it's a time you yelled or used a harsher-than-usual voice, or the time you forgot to pack your kid's lunch before sending him off to kindergarten, as I did (a few times) way back when. Maybe it happened a long time ago and you're still hanging on to guilt years later, or maybe it happened more recently and you just can't forgive yourself.

What good has that guilt done for you? What positive outcome has occurred as a result of your beating yourself up? I'll make this easy by giving you the answer: *nothing*.

Your guilt has done nothing for you other than make you feel bad about yourself. Guilt doesn't serve any purpose other than self-shaming. Seriously. It's a negative voice in our heads that tells us we're bad and wrong and we make poor decisions. That little voice wants to keep us small and safe in our comfort zones. It doesn't want us to get bigger or expand or better ourselves.

An amazing life coach named Martha Beck has a very effective exercise in which she asks you to picture that mean, inner critic as a lizard sitting on your shoulder, whispering negative things into your ear. When you picture the lizard on your shoulder, you can actually tell it to shut the hell up, or you can even just laugh at it. Separating yourself from that inner critic has the amazing effect of neutralizing that voice and helping you realize you don't have to pay attention to it. Distance yourself from that little voice and tell it, "Thank you very much, but I don't need you right now."

Step 3: Have Compassion for Yourself

Taming the guilt monster means having compassion for yourself. It's realizing that *you don't have to be perfect to be a great mom.* It's realizing that time away from the kids can be healthy, for both you and the kids. It's knowing yourself well enough to know that working is (or isn't) a necessary part of your life. It's knowing that taking care of yourself, spending time with friends, and spending time with your partner are all important and contribute to your growth and evolution.

If your friend came to you saying she feels guilty about being a working mom or about taking time to go to the gym a few times per week, what would you say to her? You would never tell your best friend she's making the wrong choices—so why would you say it to yourself? Talk to yourself the same way you would to your best friend, with kindness and compassion and empathy. We're our own worst critics, but when we put our attention outward, we're way more reasonable.

Step 4: Remember What Matters and Let Go of the Small Stuff

Do your kids feel loved? Are your kids in an environment where they're safe and protected from harm, and where they're free to grow and learn? Do you give them hugs and kisses and food and clothing and shelter? Do your kids know you're there for them, that you love them more than anything on earth? I thought so.

If your guilt is about small stuff like housework, let it go. It's okay for your house to be messy sometimes (or all the time). I literally left the beds unmade for years while raising the kids, and nothing bad happened! My kids still grew up happy and well-adjusted. It seems silly now, but I actually felt guilty about it then. What a colossal waste of time and energy to feel that way. Even when you have guests coming over, try not to sweat the housework too hard, because it just doesn't matter.

When you decide to invest time into self-care, there are going to be little things that aren't perfect as a result. Good news: You don't have to be perfect to be a great mom. Your child doesn't have to have a perfect outfit for school or a perfectly balanced healthy lunch packed each day. Your home doesn't need to be perfectly cleaned or perfectly decorated. There are so many little things in life that we turn into big things, and these things contribute to our guilt. It's small stuff; just let it go.

The goal of ditching guilt is creating more happiness and joy in your daily life. You can't feel authentic happiness and joy if you're feeling guilty about your choices, whether big or small. Guilt is unproductive and an obstacle to you living your best, most fulfilled life. Know that your choices are deeply personal and that you're doing your best and your best is good enough.

Today's To-Dos: Taming Guilt

Identify where and over what in your life you are feeling guilty. Write down all those guilt-inspiring things.

When you're finished, write the following at the top of the page: No More Guilt List. This is going to be your list of things to never feel guilty about again.

Chapter 6
YOU'RE DOING A GOOD JOB (NO, REALLY)

When a woman becomes her own best friend,
life is easier.

—*Diane von Furstenberg*

I'm a shitty mom.

I texted those words to a friend after a particularly grueling afternoon of parenting, in which I'd driven all over town to drop off and pick up my kids at various after-school activities, yelled at them more than once for being loud in the car, and basically lost my patience repeatedly. I felt so bad that my kids were stuck with me for a mom. I literally felt sorry for my children. Anyone, it seemed, would be better at the job than me.

I sat down in Sherry's office one afternoon later that week and relayed my struggles to her. I was stuck in the dark hole of my own circular, negative thoughts.

"I suck at parenting," I told her. "I'm literally the worst mom."

I leaned forward on her gray couch and noticed there were no stains or marks on it. In my house, there was not a single piece of furniture without a stain or a pen mark or, in the case of my family room bookcase, complete sentences written by my children in Sharpie, preserved forever in permanent ink.

There was evidence of my crappy parenting everywhere I looked at home and evidence of excellence everywhere else, like Sherry's office. Walking down the street, I saw moms pushing baby strollers, and the babies weren't crying. How was that even a thing? My babies always seemed to cry in the stroller. At the playground, I saw smiling moms gently lift up their toddlers to put them in the car seat, buckling them safely in for the drive home. I thought back to the hand-to-hand combat I faced trying to buckle Andrew into his car seat, how I once earned a round of applause from the moms in the playground parking lot for winning a particularly grueling round. I think I may have even pumped my fist in the air afterward, for effect. Then I got in the car and wiped the sweat off my forehead and the tears from my cheeks. *Why am I so bad at this?* It's like everyone else had an owner's manual or some secret that hadn't been shared with me. So often, I felt completely alone, like a massive failure at the one thing I really cared about doing well in life.

I outlined my list of failures to Sherry. "I let them watch too much TV," I said. "I feel like the only mom who lets her kids watch TV during the week. I really don't understand how anyone can get through a week without TV! I think it's pretty clear I'm completely messing them up for life."

Sherry observed my meltdown from her semi-reclined position in her cream-colored, ergonomically designed chair. Her slim, manicured fingers rested on a yellow pad of paper, where I noticed she wasn't writing anything down, for once. She simply sat there, listening to my laundry list of failure and shame.

"I forgot to pack Andrew's lunch yesterday. What kind of crappy mom forgets to pack her kid's lunch? Thank goodness the lunch ladies are so sweet; they gave him a school lunch for free. And I almost missed Jenna's international festival. There were probably thirty emails about it and somehow I *still* managed to forget about it, and I showed up at the very end. Matthew is being totally whiny because he wants more attention, and Jamie. Well, Jamie's so sweet I just want to cry."

Then I started crying on Sherry's couch, because *Jamie's so sweet and Matthew just wants to hang out with me and Andrew and Jenna are such great kids, and I just love them all so much and want to give them the best childhood I can, but somehow I feel like I can't get it right. No matter how much I want to get it right, I keep getting it wrong.*

These kids are innocent and beautiful, and they have everything going for them. I want to be pushing the baby stroller with the deliriously happy baby inside, smiling and cooing and making those sweet little baby sounds. I want my kid to enter the car seat willingly, without staging an all-out war. I want to be the mom who doesn't need to use television as a babysitter. I want to be good at this. I want to be better at it than I am. I want to be perfect at it. I want to be as perfect a mom as I can be, because my kids are the most perfect and beautiful little humans I've ever seen, and they deserve a mom who's perfect. And instead they're stuck with me.

Sherry continued watching, not taking notes. Finally, she spoke up.

"You know, Nina," she said, "you're allowed to be happy, even if you're not perfect. You don't have to be perfect to be a good mom. Let's start there."

Sherry and I were clearly coming at the issue from completely different points of view. She thought I could abandon the idea of perfection and instead shoot for "good enough." I knew that good enough is not what I was raised to be. I was raised to be an overachiever, a massive success. How could I lower my standards in the most important area of my life?

Perfectionism: It's a Syndrome

As women and moms, we're hard on ourselves. We hold ourselves to impossibly high standards and repeatedly find ourselves lacking, considering ourselves utter failures when we don't live up to them. We criticize ourselves and see everything we're doing wrong, rather than focusing on what we're doing right. I personally have spent an inordinate amount of time beating myself up for what I see now were minor parenting mishaps, some of which happened over twenty years ago and have been long forgotten by my kids (I hope).

Why are we as women so quick to turn on ourselves? Researchers have discovered that women uniquely suffer from perfectionism and a lack of confidence in ways that men do not, and it could be a result of experiences going back to elementary school. Girls, it turns out, are rewarded for being quiet and "good" in the classroom, while boys are more frequently reprimanded for bad behavior. As a result, boys grow up with thicker skin, more resilient and willing to take risks… while girls grow up seeking praise for being perfect.

Katty Kay and Claire Shipman, in their book *Womenomics*, studied this phenomenon, and their findings are explored in a 2014 article in *The Atlantic*:

"It's easier for young girls than for young boys to behave:…they start elementary school with a developmental edge in some key areas. They have longer attention spans, more-advanced verbal and fine-motor skills, and greater social adeptness. They generally don't charge through the halls like wild animals, or get into fights during recess. Soon they learn that they are most valuable, and most in favor, when they do things the right way: neatly and quietly."

Knowing this, we can start to shift our thought processes and develop more confidence in ourselves and our mothering. Most of us, at least the vast majority of us who are emotionally healthy and not abusers, narcissists, or other outliers, are doing our best with the information we have. So why not focus on what we're doing right, rather than what we're doing wrong?

My guess is, you're a good mom who works hard at parenting and wants only the best for her kids. When things don't work out the way you want them to, it makes you overwhelmed and frustrated—*because you want to be the best mom you can be.* You're hard on yourself when you feel like you're not delivering the perfect childhood experience, but there's no such thing.

Take yelling, for example. We've all had our moments of losing our tempers with the kids and feeling a tremendous amount of guilt after. But here's the thing—sometimes the kids don't listen, or they ignore you, or they flat-out do things they're not supposed to do. As long as kids act like kids, yelling is going to be a part of parenting. Not a single one of us has an unlimited supply of patience.

One of the problems is we each think we're the only ones who struggle with this. I watched a reality TV show in which a beautiful, young mom of five (that's right, *five*) asked her kids to help with chores she was doing around her kitchen. All these kids looked to be under ten years old. And yet, one of the kids helped set a gorgeous, antique wood table with neatly folded, white linen napkins. Another sat quietly at a spotless glass coffee table, art supplies neatly laid out, drawing pictures. Another climbed up a wooden step-stool to place a ceramic vase of perfectly arranged flowers on a shelf in the white, open-concept, dream kitchen. All the while, the mom spoke warmly in the voice-over about how deeply she loves it when her kids help around the house. At no point did any of the kids pitch a fit and scream, "I don't want to," nor were any crushed Goldfish crackers or juice boxes spilled on the floor or the couch (incredibly, there were no snacks or drinks or any other bribery tools in sight), nor were any tears shed at any point, by either the kids or the mom. I watched this scene with a mixture of fascination, confusion, and repulsion. It was idyllic *and completely unrealistic.*

Depictions like this one are harmful because they're a fantasy. They further reinforce our perfectionistic standards and make us feel like failures at parenthood, because scenes like this are simply impossible to realize in our own homes. It's like looking at a picture of a supermodel in a magazine—an image that's totally airbrushed and photoshopped, nothing to do with reality, and completely unattainable. But we look at the picture and think we're actually supposed to look that way, smooth, unlined, clear-skinned, and cellulite-free. And we beat ourselves up when we don't.

Real life is messy. We yell, we scream, we cry, sometimes all three on the same day. Our kids don't listen, our kitchens aren't clean, and sometimes we lose our patience. Goldfish crackers end up on the floor and all over our furniture—juice boxes spill all over the seats of our cars.

Knowing that, what if we decided to love and accept and approve of ourselves anyway? What if we decided to accept that despite the mess and the spills and the messed-up furniture and the kids who talk back sometimes, *we're still doing an amazing job at being a mom?*

Your kids are flawed and human and imperfect, and yet you love and accept and approve of them. You forgive them no matter what they do, because you love them and because you know they're still learning and growing and evolving. You don't just forgive them—you cheer them on and encourage them, letting them know that being imperfect is being human. You tell them they are doing a good job and that they are great.

Why can't you offer this same gift to yourself?

Your Best, Flaws and All, Is Great

A big part of this is understanding that *the perfect is the enemy of the good.*

When we expect ourselves to be perfect parents, we're setting ourselves up for failure, with an all-or-nothing mentality that tells us that anything less than perfection is unacceptable. You can never live up to the standard you're setting for yourself, if the standard is perfection. So rather than aiming for perfection, aim to do your best, whatever that looks like, and give yourself plenty of approval for doing so.

When my son Matt was in middle school, he was incredibly hard on himself when it came to his academics. He has a highly sensitive nature, and on the rare occasions when he received an A-, or God forbid a grade in the B range, he was devastated and inconsolable, thinking himself a failure. He had absorbed the *all-or-nothing* mentality, thinking that he's either perfect or a failure. It was either black or white, good or bad, with no in between. Sadly, he probably learned that from me.

I told him to relax. "Shoot for a B," I told him. His quest for, and expectation of, perfection in his grades was no longer serving him. It was making him anxious and depressed, and taking the fun out of his middle school years. It was time to realize there's lots of room to do a good job, somewhere in the middle between perfection and failure. It was time to let good enough be okay. It's not about lowering standards—it's about knowing you're still okay, no matter what your grade is.

The same lesson applies to us as moms. Shooting for perfection doesn't serve us because perfection is not possible when it comes to motherhood. The job is simply too messy, too unpredictable, and too enormous. Letting go of perfection allows us to exhale and let good enough be sufficient. It allows us to dwell in that middle place, somewhere in between feeling like a failure and feeling like we're perfect, where we know we're doing our best and we know our kids are thriving despite our inevitable missteps.

We're all doing our best with the information and experience we have right now. The most important thing we can do is to give our kids a really good childhood, one with predominantly positive memories, one in which your child feels loved and cherished every day.

Thinking you're a crappy mother doesn't make you a better mom. In fact, the opposite is true. When you're hard on yourself and thinking negative thoughts about yourself, you're more apt to be short-tempered, impatient, and just generally unpleasant. So if you want to be the best mom you can be, stop being hard on yourself and start to accept and approve of yourself.

When we learn to accept our best efforts, to love ourselves and approve of ourselves, we can experience more joy and happiness in our lives. The good news is, accepting and approving of ourselves is simply a matter of changing our thoughts. And thoughts are surprisingly easy to change, once you decide.

Follow these steps next time you start beating yourself up and thinking you're not good enough:

1. Notice the thoughts as they come.

This first step is probably the most challenging, because it requires you to be aware of your own thought patterns, rather than simply allowing your thoughts to flow naturally, as you're probably accustomed to doing. As soon as you start to think negative thoughts about yourself, notice yourself doing so. Catch yourself in the act. That way you can do something about it.

2. Separate yourself from the thoughts.

Realize that your thoughts are not you. You are the one observing the thoughts. The thoughts come from the fear center of your brain, a place that wants to be negative. Your true inner voice—your intuition—is much kinder and gentler than the thought stream running through your head. So make a decision not to attach to the thoughts—simply observe them and let them pass.

3. Remind yourself of what's true.

Replace the negative thought with a more positive, and truthful, one. For example, if your thoughts are saying you're the worst mom ever because you missed your kid's poetry reading at school, let that thought go and remind yourself that you're a great mom, you're doing your best, and there is no single person alive who doesn't make mistakes or mess up sometimes…and that maybe you need to write yourself a little note in your planner to remind yourself next time. If you're having trouble coming up with a positive statement, think of what you'd say to your best friend or your daughter if she were in the same situation.

Once you start to replace your negative thoughts with positive ones, you'll be shocked at how much lighter you feel. By observing and changing your thoughts, you empower yourself to move forward with a more positive mindset and to intelligently approach solving your parenting challenges.

Today's To-Dos: You're Doing Great

To-Do #1

Practice approving of yourself. Take time at the end of each day to write down five things you did or said that you're proud of.

Use this format or something similar that works for you:

1. Today I: _____ and it was the right thing to do.

2. Today I: _____ and it was the right thing to do.

3. Today I: _____ and
   it was the right thing to do.

4. Today I: _____ and
   it was the right thing to do.

5. Today I: _____ and
   it was the right thing to do.

To-Do #2

You have so many amazing attributes that other people can see, but I bet you don't spend much time celebrating those attributes.
List five things you love about your appearance:

1.

2.

3.

4.

5.

List five things you love about your body:

1.

2.

3.

4.

5.

List five things you love about your personality:

1.

2.

3.

4.

5.

Now, list ten reasons your kids are fortunate to have you as a mom:

1.

2.

3.

4.

5.

6.

7.

8.

9.

10.

Now, every time you start to feel insecure, interrupt that thought and think about the things on this list. Feel how you're succeeding as a person and as a mom. You've spent so much time beating yourself up...so spend a few minutes each day lifting yourself up and celebrating your successes and victories.

Chapter 7

PERMISSION

*What would happen if one woman told the truth
about her life? The world would split open.*

—MURIEL RUKEYSER

Is this even allowed?
I was in a dark studio during my introductory pole dance class when I first learned *the walk*, a slow-moving, flowing, draggy, and incredibly liberating movement.

The teacher's voice, dripping with sensuality, filled the space as we walked at a painfully slow pace, single file, in a wide circle around the studio. "Move sloooooooowly. Drag your foot behind you, stick your booty out, shoulders back, push your breasts forward. Take up space. Let your hands move over your body, savor every inch of your beautiful curves."

Struggling to keep my balance in my six-inch platform shoes while walking as slowly as possible without falling over, I pushed my hips out to the side with each step forward. Rather than my usual posture, standing straight with everything sucked in, I exhaled and let it all out, letting my hands move from my waist down and around my curves. I'm not going to lie; it was awkward at first. But that feeling didn't last. Very quickly, my body started to feel how natural this type of movement was. It felt like my body *wanted* to move this way, like it hadn't been allowed to until now.

I felt naughty, savoring a forbidden, previously abandoned piece of myself that hadn't seen daylight in years. It felt like I was doing something against the rules, that everyone would say was wrong, especially for a mother of four. I'd been raised, like many of us, whispering secretly with my friends about sex. You weren't allowed to talk about it out loud, or your parents might hear you and then you'd be in trouble. I was interested in sex when I was younger, in the feelings and the power it seemed to hold, but exploring it seemed impossible. Any hint of discussion was deemed inappropriate in my Italian Catholic family. All this secrecy forces sexuality to be a part of our lives that's hidden away. By the time I learned the walk in the dance studio, that part of me was so small that it was barely discernible.

But moving this way felt like freedom, like suddenly unearthing a delicious secret living inside my body, one that had been there all along but had been completely buried, neglected, and forgotten. I suddenly wanted this secret to live freely in my body, not just in the studio but outside as well. I felt an overwhelming sense of not just *wanting* but *needing* this movement in my life. It was clear, with a confidence that permeated my entire body, that need being fulfilled was an imperative to my life and future happiness.

In this room, it wasn't just allowed, it was encouraged. Finally, it was okay to walk and dance and play without inhibitions, without external societal judgements on what was considered acceptable behavior. What pole dance gave me wasn't simply a host of challenging pole dance moves—it gave me *permission* to explore the hidden parts of me that society told me to shut down.

I Needed Permission. You Need Permission.

Society tells us not to be outwardly sexual beings. Sexuality is often seen as taboo and relegated to the privacy of the bedroom. But the societal limitations many of us feel in our lives go way beyond sexuality. Society tells us to keep our anger under control lest we be perceived as shrill or, worse, bitchy. It tells us to keep our opinions to ourselves. Society encourages us to conform to certain standards of behavior, to be appropriate, stay inside a box that keeps us small and forces us to renounce huge parts of our being in the service of making sure everyone else is comfortable.

What else does society tell us? Society tells us to give up everything for our kids, to put ourselves last in service to them, lest we be perceived as selfish. *Good moms don't take time for themselves. Good moms sacrifice themselves. Good moms give up everything for their families.*

But what if we gave ourselves permission to be true to ourselves, not just in the privacy of our bedrooms and our homes, but out in the world for everyone to see? What if we were to embrace our sensuality, our rage, our bitchiness, our intelligence, and our ambition, and wear those qualities as outwardly as we wear our kindness and our nurturing and our thoughtfulness? What if giving ourselves permission was another step toward getting us on that to-do list?

Think about the fact that we give permission to everyone else: our kids, our partners, our friends. We sign actual permission slips for our children. When we give advice to our friends, we're *giving them permission* to make the choices they want to make. But often we hold ourselves back from giving ourselves permission to do what we want to do or be who we want to be.

In fact, when we first become moms, we relegate huge portions of our lives to our personal dustbins. It feels natural at first, when we fall in love with our tiny little baby and he needs us so much. Everything else falls away. It feels like falling in love, like you and your beloved baby only need each other—you don't need your spouse or food or water or anything else. This process is totally normal and natural; it's nature's way of ensuring we'll stick around and care for our new babies.

But think of a pie that's been divided into slices. Before you have kids, you have all these different slices that are elements of your life. You have work and friends and social life and family and spiritual life and hobbies and interests. Plus, you have your romantic life, your sexual life, your physical health, and your emotional life.

When you have a baby, you and that baby become the entire pie. Your entire focus shifts to your baby and her needs.

The problem comes when you continue to live this way indefinitely. You contain a multitude of dimensions, all of which deserve to see the light of day. Your emotional life, your spiritual life, your sexual life, and all the other slices of your personal pie, all these parts of you need air time.

Maybe it's because of society's expectations of us, or maybe it's because of expectations we put on ourselves, but we all get into ruts where we're solely focused on our kids, to the exclusion of everything else. And sometimes we think it's because we're not allowed to let those parts of our lives back in. Doing so feels selfish, like we're neglecting our responsibilities.

It's easy to fall into this trap and martyr ourselves. It may be hard to admit it, but we can get a secondary benefit from doing so. There's a sense of superiority that comes from being willing to sacrifice literally everything for your kids. Especially in our culture, where parenting is practically a competitive sport, those of us who are willing to sacrifice everything else to be the best at it can derive a certain sense of satisfaction from doing so.

Here's the problem with that sacrifice—we ignore that we are women, not just moms. Let's give ourselves permission to step back from the hyper-parenting and the martyrdom and look at our lives objectively. Who are we, really? We're moms, yes, but who else?

We may be:

A spouse or partner

A daughter and/or a sister

A boss or an employee

A friend or mentor

And beyond that, take a moment to ask yourself: Who am I beyond all those roles? What am I passionate about? Reading or knitting or dancing? Maybe you love running or Pilates or having sex for hours. Is political news your thing or true crime podcasts or cooking gourmet meals? Give yourself permission to let those parts back in and be who you are, who you were before you became a mom. Putting yourself back on the to-do list means giving yourself permission to retrieve and reclaim your hidden parts.

I Just Can't Decide

Sometimes we tell ourselves stories in order to avoid making a decision that might be uncomfortable. How often have you heard a friend bemoan the fact that she "just can't decide" what to do about a particular situation? Maybe she just can't decide whether to go back to work, or whether to move across the country, or whether to get a divorce. I've found that "I just can't decide" is often what we tell ourselves when the truth is "I know what I want, but I don't know if it's okay to want it."

What we generally mean when we say that is "I don't know if it's socially acceptable." Not deciding avoids any chance of being wrong. How many times have you thought: *I'm afraid I'll be an outcast? I'm afraid they'll think I'm irresponsible or lazy or crazy or bitchy or slutty?* Or whatever other stories you're telling yourself.

What we really mean with all these swirling thoughts is "I want to, but I haven't given myself permission."

Often as we try to make decisions, we're just afraid to be "that mom"—the one with the pole in her house, for example. Or the one who gets divorced. The one who sells her home and moves her family to New Zealand. The one who goes back to school to earn her master's degree at forty-five. The one who quits her corporate 9-to-5 job to start her own gluten-free bake shop. The one who ignores the "rules" and decides to forge ahead on her own path. Women who go against the grain like this are on the other side of a line that many of us choose never to cross.

There is something amazing that lies on the other side of that decision line: *freedom.* If you have the courage to give yourself permission to live authentically, you'll have access to a whole world of experiences, with the vast potential for joy and fulfillment that doesn't exist inside society's boundaries and rules.

Once we decide, once and for all, *yes, it's allowed; yes, I have permission to do what I want to do; yes, I'm going to be exactly who I am,* we have the freedom to let go of society's shackles and truly live our lives.

Whether you're in the throes of a mom-life crisis and longing to live more authentically, or even if you're just overwhelmed by your to-do list and wanting to find more time for yourself, there is very little chance of doing so without giving yourself permission. I would go so far as to say it's not going to happen without permission.

Realizing this is challenging, I have something that might help you. I have written four big permission slips. Use them! I want you to embrace them and live them and let them get embedded deep inside you.

You have permission to be imperfect.

I harbor a deep suspicion that even those moms who act all perfect all the time, who dress their kids in matching clothes and hang out in front of school with a clipboard so they can get you to sign up for PTA stuff, are really insecure messes when they're home and no one is looking.

We're all just living our lives each day, doing our best, and trying to get it right. Every one of us is looking around at the other moms and thinking they have some kind of secret to doing it right. They don't! Every one of us is faking it some of the time, on some level. Your empathy toward other moms, and yourself, will improve when you give yourself permission to be flawed and imperfect, because it will help you realize we're *all* flawed and imperfect. Even *that* mom.

You have permission to be who you are, to live authentically and wholly in your truth, whatever that looks like.

If that means taking pole dance classes in order to rediscover your sensuality, do it. *You have permission.* If that means moving across the country because it's what you want to do, do it. If that means leaving a flatlined marriage where there's no hope for happiness in the future, do it. If that means changing careers, or giving up your career, or starting a brand new business, do it. Wanting to do it is enough reason. You don't need society's permission to live your truth. "Society" is not handing out permission slips, unfortunately. You have to give it to yourself.

There are a few caveats to this of course, such as, be who you are as long as you aren't harming others, physically or emotionally. Aside from that, there is only one you, and you're the only one with your unique combination of strengths and talents and experiences. You have precious little time here on earth. There is not one minute to waste living a life that doesn't thrill you.

You have permission to take care of yourself every day and treat yourself with as much love and care as you treat your child(ren).

At a conference I attended, my friend Linda brought all her own vegetarian food in an insulated bag. In addition, she brought a separate insulated case filled with organic spices and seasonings. At lunchtime each day of the seminar, she prepared herself a perfectly seasoned little feast, which she followed up by brushing and flossing her teeth. This woman loved herself hard! When I asked her about it, she unapologetically replied, *"I worship myself."*

I think of her often. How many of us have ever uttered those three words together, out loud?

I worship myself.

You may not be the type to lug your spices and seasonings across the country to business conferences, but there are other ways to worship yourself. One way to get started is by reminding yourself of this important concept: *your needs matter*—dietary needs or some other type of need. Meeting them starts with deciding they matter just as much as everyone else's and you are allowed to give yourself permission to fulfill those needs.

Create your own self-care permission slip to accomplish this. Your permission slip could address a tiny self-care need or a larger life-altering one.

Giving yourself permission is advocating for yourself. It's about saying, *I'm important enough to merit some consideration in this family.* I'm the hub of the wheel of this family unit, and I need to keep myself healthy and happy in order to keep it running smoothly.

When you give yourself permission to be who you are and do what you need to do to be your best, you also give other women permission to do the same. You're modeling that behavior not just for your friends and acquaintances, but also for your daughters and sons. Giving yourself permission benefits everyone in your orbit.

You have permission to let go of commitments you've made to yourself that no longer serve you.

You may be holding on to certain limiting beliefs or behaviors or commitments that are holding you back in life. Give yourself permission to let go of those that are no longer aligned with who you are and what you really want.

For example, there was a period when I wanted to start a content-based website. I bought a domain name and interviewed web designers and assembled lists of various types of content. I envisioned the site as having loads of articles with tips and advice, fun and interesting and relatable pieces to help moms feel supported and like part of a community.

But building a new site takes time, energy, and creativity. I became overwhelmed. The new website started taking my focus away from my "day job" at *momAgenda*, so I had less time to focus on the work that was actually putting food on the table. In addition, I was getting more and more distracted at home, thinking about my new project.

For a moment I was distraught. What was I going to do? I'm a follow-through person. When I start something, I see it through to completion. I felt this project was no exception. But at the same time, it felt crazy to start a new site amid all the other things I had going on in my life.

I finally realized that a content-based website was a fun idea but I didn't have the time or energy to dedicate to it. *I gave myself permission to quit.* That decision was so liberating! I walked away from the content-based site and never looked back. And that's how I know it was the right decision. I felt liberated, unencumbered, and like things were right in my world again.

What do you have going on in your world that's no longer serving you? Do you have projects or beliefs that are taking up time and energy but not really furthering your goals and dreams? Or do you have projects that you simply don't want to do anymore? If so, *you have permission to quit.*

There are so many forces in our society telling us we have to work hard, to persevere, to push through challenges. And sometimes we do. We have challenges in our marriages, challenges in parenting, challenges at work, and those challenges are worth the hard work and energy and time it takes to improve them.

But there are also situations in which things are hard and there isn't really any upside to continuing. Like a project that's just distracting you from your real priorities. Or a belief that's keeping you stuck in a negative mindset. Those are the things to quit. Walk away and don't look back.

Today's To-Dos: Permission

To-Do #1

Your Needs Matter!

Take out your journal and write for a few minutes about any needs you have that are currently not being met. Make sure to consider:

- ✧ Your unmet *emotional* needs (these are needs related to your inner life, such as the need for intimacy or closeness with your partner, the need for romance, or the need for alone time to recharge).

- ✧ Your unmet *physical* needs (these are needs related to your physical body—think your health, fitness, food, and nutrition).

- ✧ Your unmet *spiritual* needs (these are needs related to a higher power, or to your personal growth journey).

- ✧ Your unmet *personal* needs (these are needs that are unique and specific to you—maybe you need to listen to music or garden or read or create art).

To-Do #2

Projects or Ideas That Are No Longer Serving You

Think about everything you have going on in your life and consider whether there are any projects or belief systems that are no longer serving you. These can be outdated commitments you've made to yourself or belief systems carried from childhood that are no longer relevant.

Write them down in your journal. Whenever you feel ready, write yourself a permission slip to let them go.

Chapter 8

OVERCOMING OVERWHELM

*It's precisely those who are busiest who most need
to give themselves a break.*

—*Pico Iyer*

As I walked through one of the hundreds of glass doors and gazed up and around the space, I caught my breath. It was May 2005. I'd never been inside a building this vast and open. The Jacob Javits Center in Manhattan, the site of the annual National Stationery Show, was filled to capacity with vendor booths displaying cards, notebooks, planners, pens, wrapping papers, photo albums, and all sorts of pretty office supplies. Buyers slowly made their way up and down each of the vast walkways lined with booths, peering inside each one so they wouldn't miss a thing as they searched for their next great find. Others huddled in the hallways, waiting impatiently for their turn to speak with vendors and make purchases for their stores back at home. There must have been thousands of booths, and many more thousands of people milling about the space.

I launched *momAgenda* at the National Stationery Show at the Javits Center that spring. Over the course of those three days, we sold out of our entire inventory, receiving orders for 6,000 units from 120 stores. The excitement never slowed down during those three days, with a constant stream of store buyers in our booth. It was overwhelming, exhilarating, and exciting to see my "baby" succeed in the real world.

At the end of the show, the excitement over and reality beginning to set in, my sister and I packed up. As I placed my sample planners in a plastic box, I started to feel over-whelmed. I sat down on a plastic folding chair and, out of nowhere, started hysterically crying.

"What's the matter?" my sister asked. "You just had the most amazing show ever. Why are you crying?"

"Because I don't know what to do!" I blubbered, tears streaming down my face.

I didn't know what I had gotten myself into. I believed in my product line, and I had fun developing it but was not at all prepared for it to succeed out in the real world and actually become a viable business.

At the time I had two kids in elementary school, one in preschool, and one who was still a baby. I was terrified that I was going to lose control of mothering them. What if I got so busy that I started missing important events in their lives? What if I didn't get to take them to school and pick them up and chaperone field trips? What if I had to go on business trips that would take me away from the kids for days at a time? What if that started to be okay with me? What if the kids started to like their babysitter more than me? What if starting this company made me a completely different mom than the one I wanted to be, and now that the train was out of the station, there was no way to stop it?

I met a woman, around that same time, who had flown into New York from California. A popular and well-known blogger, she was considered an expert and mentor to women entrepreneurs, and had flown in specifically to judge a new business contest in which I was competing. The contest was a big deal, a showdown of ten leading female entrepreneurs launching promising new startups, and sponsored by several large companies. I was honored to be chosen as one of those female entrepreneurs in the competition (spoiler: I didn't win). She and I chatted, and she mentioned that it happened to be her daughter's birthday that day.

"Oh fun! Is your daughter here with you?" I asked.

She shook her head. "No," she replied. "She's back home in California. It sucks, but this opportunity was too good to pass up. She's bummed out, but she'll be okay. Her dad's there with her."

This conversation caused all the blood in my body to rush up to my face. I felt the little pinpricks of anxiety all through my body. *What if this happens to me?* I thought. *What if I miss my kid's birthday just to judge some stupid contest that no one's going to care about a year from now?*

(Just a note here to say I don't judge anyone who makes this choice! My point is that this is not what I wanted, nor what was right for me, and I knew it, and that made me feel anxious and overwhelmed.)

There was so much anxiety flooding my body that it didn't even occur to me in that moment that starting a company meant having the freedom to make those types of choices. That woman was an independent, work-from-home blogger—she was her own boss and ran her own business. She could have chosen to decline the opportunity to judge the contest and stay home for her daughter's birthday, but she wanted to be there at the show. It was her decision. But I wasn't rational in the moment of my crying spree. All I felt was fear. I started the business because I wanted freedom, but when the business took off so quickly, it felt like that freedom might inadvertently slip away.

On top of the anxiety I was feeling on a personal level, I felt work-related anxiety. The company had taken off without my anticipating it. I'd purposefully kept my expectations low going into the trade show, so that I wouldn't be disappointed if we only sold a handful of planners. I figured I'd go back home to Connecticut and start selling my day planners at the preschool moms' night out and the elementary school book fair, and my life wouldn't really change. I hadn't even thought about putting systems in place to run an actual company or hiring people to help.

But now I had orders from stores all over the country for 6,000 day planners. I had to figure out a way to ship the right planners to the right stores without messing up. I barely knew the difference between UPS and USPS. And I had to bill all these people! I felt certain I was going to be spending the rest of my life packing and shipping boxes from my dining room table while my kids cried due to their loneliness in the other room. I was already a failure in my own mind, and I'd barely started.

This was complete and total overwhelm. But it wasn't simply overwhelm. It was overwhelm that bordered on panic. After the show was over, I went home and got to work. But the stress was there. I started doing awful things like lashing out inappropriately and skipping out on commitments in order to stay home and stare at the TV. I was overwhelmed, and that blocked me from focusing. The fact that I was doing *everything* meant I wasn't doing *anything* particularly well. There was too much on my plate to succeed in any area. Not to mention I handled tasks that weren't anywhere near my wheelhouse and failed on every level. Doing everything wasn't just overwhelming, it was completely ineffective.

Everyday Overwhelm

Sometimes we have existential, I-just-started-a-company-and-I-don't-know-what-to-do-type overwhelm, but more frequently we suffer from more garden-variety, everyday overwhelm. This is the overwhelm that leads to total exhaustion. You've got kids, work, household responsibilities, friends, too much to remember and do, and not enough time to do it all. It could take one of any number of different forms, but the general formula is, you have too much of *something* or *lots of things* and not enough time for *everything else that's important.*

Too much to do = no time or energy to hug kids/notice spouse's existence/eat food/attend to your own needs/enjoy life.

Part of the problem is that being "crazy busy!" has become a badge of honor among moms (and maybe among a majority of people in our culture). As moms, our kids' needs can seem endless, and we pride ourselves on meeting their every need and then some. We equate busyness with goodness. The thinking goes, the busier you are, the better the mom you are. And though we don't always want to admit it, we all want to be supermom in our own ways, if being supermom means being the best mom we can be to our kids.

We purposefully (or subconsciously) fill our lives with stuff that takes up all our time, and then we get stressed out that we don't have time to do the things we really enjoy doing.

Time is perceived as scarce. The truth is, we have time for whatever we put our focus on. The idea that if we decide we're no longer going to run the PTA fundraiser or cook gourmet meals or spend two hours helping our kids with homework, the whole world is going to fall apart is really something we have to disabuse ourselves of. The world is going to keep on spinning no matter what you do, so you might as well live the life you really want.

How we spend our days is, of course, how we spend our lives.—Annie Dillard

Keeping that in mind, if you're ready to drop the "crazy busy, so exhausted" story and reduce your overwhelm, you'll start thinking more carefully about the commitments you take on. Time is not an infinite resource. Do you really want to spend a sizable chunk of that time, and therefore your life, doing a single thing you don't want to do or need to do?

Neither do I.

Eight Ways to Take Back Your Time and Decrease Overwhelm

1. Urgent vs. Important: Learn to Discern

When there are a million different things pulling you in a million different directions, when you're running around like a crazy person and living in chaos, it can be challenging to stop to figure out where you actually need to focus your attention. It's easy to lose track of what's important. Small issues can seem bigger than they really are, and big issues can slip through the cracks. It becomes tempting to focus on the squeaky wheel, the person in your life who yells the loudest, whose needs appear to be the most urgent.

Living like this is reactive, and it's ineffective in terms of getting you what you really want. When you live this way, you're letting outside forces—basically, whoever screams the loudest or asks the most persuasively—dictate where you're placing your focus. It's important to take steps to reduce overwhelm so that you're not living reactively.

There's an old saying: "Urgent things are seldom important, and important things are seldom urgent." Try to focus on what is truly important to you and ignore the problem or person that is screaming the loudest. When you can discern between the two, life becomes less overwhelming since you'll be able to place your focus on what's important to you.

2. Do the Next Right Thing

When we're trying to get through something difficult, an effective approach is taking things one day at a time. Doing the next right thing is even more precise and effective. It's a notion that's grounded in the present moment. The concept exists to help you to keep your focus in the here and now, breaking down overwhelming tasks into smaller chunks and, in doing so, making life more manageable.

When you're making one of the thousands of decisions you need to make each day, when life gets busy and overwhelming, when everything feels chaotic and pulling you in multiple directions, the solution is to stop. Breathe. Instead of reacting, try to pause and think. Then, *do the next right thing.* Put one foot in front of the other, and then do it again. String together a whole bunch of "next right things" and you can accomplish more than if you focus on the larger task, because you'll feel less overwhelmed.

It helps me to take a step back, make a list of what needs to be done, consider my priorities, and then decide what to do next—what are the small next right things. Pausing rather than reacting provides clarity and helps block out the Greek chorus impacting your choices.

3. Think Small: Take Baby Steps

When you're feeling overwhelmed, any task, however small, can feel monumental. I remember sitting at my desk shortly after that trade show, trying to put systems in place to build a company to support my little product. My head was spinning at the enormity of the task ahead of me. It was too much to think about, so I decided to stop thinking about it and focus my attention solely on what I had to do *that day*. In order to build this business into something really big, I needed to think really small. Like, baby small. It needed to be so easy, I wouldn't be afraid to do it. I needed to take baby steps each day in order to make accomplishing my goal more manageable.

Today, I'm going to interview one web designer.

Today, I'm going to write the copy for the marketing postcard.

Today, I'm going to visit a local store customer to see if they need more product.

It took practice and discipline to keep my focus small, but it worked. Every day, I'd do what I had to do that day, and not attempt to do anything else or even *think* about anything else. Then the next day, I repeated my system. I made sure to keep the tasks baby small so that each day would feel easy, sometimes even enjoyable, rather than overwhelming. Over time, I strung together a series of days in which I'd accomplished a couple of small things.

Six months later, when Katie Couric held up a crocodile-embossed, deep-maroon-red *momAgenda* Desktop on the *Today Show* one early December morning and announced, "This helps moms get organized," and the website was deluged with so many orders that we feared it might crash (spoiler: it didn't), we were ready.

4. Delegation and Letting Go

Shortly after that fateful day at the trade show, I wasn't afraid to admit it: I needed expertise I didn't have. It was time to bring in a partner, someone who could focus on the day-today tasks and excel at them. Fortunately, the ideal person was already in my life as a friend, neighbor, and fellow mom. Maureen became chief operating officer and eventually my business partner, and bringing her in was among the best and most important decisions I made as president of *momAgenda*.

Asking for help can be challenging, because it means relinquishing a certain amount of control. We've all had the experience of leaving our kids with a babysitter or a relative and wanting to micromanage their every move. But delegating tasks means letting go and letting someone else handle them.

Step one to effective delegating is to identify the things you're good at, the things you enjoy doing, and/or the things that are most important to you.

Step two is to be okay with letting someone else handle the rest of the stuff that needs doing. I wanted to oversee all creative aspects of the business, for example. I wasn't interested in learning to code and design an entire e-commerce website by myself. But I wanted control over the look and feel of the products, the website, and the marketing campaigns.

When you stop micromanaging and start to focus your energy primarily on the things that are particularly important to you, and delegate or simply let go of everything else, you eliminate the unnecessary clutter that's taking up space in your mind. In doing so, you create space for what matters most to you.

I could have held on to total control of *momAgenda* and micromanaged every aspect of it, but I didn't want to. My home life and sanity would have suffered. It was scary, deciding to release control. It turned out that Maureen was not only smarter than me, but also much better at the tasks I delegated to her than I ever could have been.

Ultimately, the business became successful beyond anything I had ever imagined. And I still got to pick up my kids from school and go to all the parent-teacher conferences and chaperone the field trips. I got to be the mom I wanted to be because I let go of control over the company.

5. Don't Be Afraid to Ask for (and Accept) Help

It's challenging to admit we need help when we've built our entire lives around the idea that we are perfect supermoms who can do it all. As moms and managers (or comanagers) of our homes, we're reluctant to ask for help, and the list of reasons is seemingly endless. We feel it's a sign of weakness or a sign that we're really not up to the task. We think no one else can do the job as well as we can. We think that it would take as much energy to explain the task as it would to simply do the task, so we might as well just do it ourselves. We think it's easier to do it ourselves than bear the inevitable disappointment when someone else lets us down by not doing it the way we want them to. We think they might say no if we ask, and we don't want to hear the word no. We think we have to be self-sufficient and handle it ourselves—we made the decision to have kids; therefore, we must bear the burden of all the work that comes with them.

In short, we sacrifice ourselves at the altar of motherhood, making ourselves exhausted and miserable in the process. We martyr ourselves, deciding we are all alone in the universe, and we end up resenting our partners or others in our lives who we feel are not there for us. But the reason they're not there for us is because *we won't let them be there for us*!

As my business grew, I knew I also needed a little more help from the people in my life, to make things at home run smoothly. It took me a while to realize it, but I figured out something interesting about leaning on others.

Asking for help is a sign of strength.

It takes a tremendous amount of courage to be vulnerable enough to admit you can't do it all yourself. Asking for help is a sign that you know your own limits and you're willing to honor them. Asking for help is a form of self-care.

The great irony about asking for help is that it's actually a gift to the person you're asking. So many people welcome the opportunity to be helpers: friends, parents/in-laws, siblings, paid professionals like babysitters and cleaners, and even your kids. It's empowering to them and gives them the opportunity to make you happy. It makes them feel good to be asked, and it makes you feel good to accept the help.

Once you ask for it, be willing to accept it. Open yourself up to receiving this gift of help. This means taking your hands off the wheel, releasing control, and letting the other person do their thing in their way. Let it be okay if they don't do it exactly the way you would. If your partner loads the dishwasher, please don't rearrange it because you think your way of loading it is better. If your babysitter folds the laundry and puts it away, just enjoy the moment rather than caving to your desire to refold it properly. They may not do it perfectly—but we're no longer trying to be perfect; we're just looking for good enough. Sit back, release control, and enjoy having one less thing on your plate.

Exhale. It feels good, doesn't it?

6. Automate

A Cornell University study reveals that each day, we make two hundred decisions about food. Just food. We make literally thousands of decisions each day about everything in our lives. Overwhelm occurs when we have too many things to do, decisions to make, errands to run, friends to call, bills to pay. To automate means to make something automatic—to make it something you can do without even thinking. When you begin to practice automation, you'll actually reduce the amount of decisions you need to make each day and help simplify your life.

I've automated my wardrobe by choosing an outfit for each season and wearing it just about every day. In the summer, I live in sundresses. And in colder weather, I wear jeans, a T-shirt, and boots. I have a million white T-shirts! Automating this one small decision creates space in my brain for more important considerations, like what to eat for breakfast.

Speaking of breakfast...you can automate that too. Eat the same thing for breakfast and lunch each day, so you only need to apply decision-making brainpower to dinner.

Speaking of dinner...you can semiautomate dinner too. Create a list of fifteen to twenty easy weeknight meals that you and the kids enjoy, and put them on rotation. Use a meal planning pad or app and schedule your meals for the week or even the entire month. Order your groceries and watch the magic happen.

You can automate by setting up auto ship for household supplies like paper towels, laundry detergent, toilet paper, and napkins. I have mine set up to ship to me every two months, and now I rarely have to think about running to the store for household items.

Another way to automate is to establish routines. For example, you may choose to go to the same yoga class every Monday, Wednesday, and Friday. This eliminates the need to agonize over your schedule each day trying to figure out when you're going to find time to work out.

Automate your daily routine so that you don't have to think too hard about what you're doing each day. I have a set morning routine that involves coffee and a workout. Then I do actual work until lunchtime. I created a rule for myself: I don't book any meetings, appointments, or coffee dates in the mornings—that way I know I'll have time to get all my work done each day. After lunch is for meetings, appointments, and, of course, driving my kids all over town for their after-school activities.

Automate your social media and other communications so that you don't get sucked in throughout your day. This will help you avoid massive time sucks. Yes, I'm looking at you, Facebook, Instagram, and Twitter! Make rules for yourself about social media so you don't blow hours per day scrolling endlessly. My personal time sinkhole is Instagram, so I made a rule for myself to only check first thing in the morning, while drinking my coffee, and at the end of the day, before bed.

Check email three times per day: morning, lunchtime, and at the end of the day. *This one rule will save you an enormous amount of time each day.*

I recommend you identify your favorite distractions and set a time limit for them. A few come to mind, in addition to social media, including checking emails, watching television, and mindlessly surfing the internet for articles about whatever issue you're having in life that day. Set a timer on your phone and when the timer goes off, turn it off.

Automating leaves you more brainpower for the big things, like whether to move or change jobs or have a baby. It's one of my most important practices for keeping overwhelm at a manageable level.

7. Make Lists

At the beginning of each week make a list of all the things you need to get done over the course of the week. I like to do this on Sunday nights. I spend about half an hour with my day planner, planning the week ahead. Part of this process is scheduling in workouts and school pickups and other appointments. The other part is making a list of everything I need to do.

Once you've made this list, consider what absolutely must get done versus what can wait or be crossed off. What can be delegated, pushed till next week, or simply eliminated? What can be automated? The goal is to make this to-do list as short and sweet as you possibly can, so you'll have more time to enjoy life, hug your kids, and notice your spouse's existence.

Most important, go easy on yourself. Don't pressure yourself to do everything on the list. Do your best to get through it.

8. Say No

There's an entire chapter of this book devoted to my favorite word, *no,* but it's important to mention here because using it helps us overcome overwhelm. When we're overwhelmed, it's because we've said yes to more than we can handle.

Many of us think we can't say no, and the reasons can be complicated. Mostly it has to do with wanting to be "nice" to others. I'm going to gently suggest that at this point, it's more important to be nice to yourself. In addition, is it really nice to say yes when you really want to say no? Is it nice to say yes and then resent the person who made the request? Is it nice to say yes and then be seething afterward because you really don't want the extra responsibility?

It's time to redefine nice. Being nice doesn't mean saying something sweet but inauthentic in the moment. Being nice means doing what's best for you and your family. And if taking on a particular commitment makes you anything less than ecstatic, then it's not nice to say yes to it.

Remember those shoulds? Often we say yes to things not because we want to do them, but because we think we "should." When we get rid of the shoulds, we're left with doing things because we want to do them, rather than because we feel obligated. As a result, we do less, but accomplish more. We spend time with fewer people but have higher quality relationships. We avoid overwhelm because we're discerning about how we're spending our time.

Today's To-Dos: Overcoming Overwhelm
Spend the next week noting areas where you're micromanaging. List them here:

_____

_____

_____

_____

What can you delegate in your home?

_____

_____

_____

What can you delegate with regard to your kids?

_____

_____

_____

_____

What can you delegate in your workplace?

_____

_____

_____

What can you automate in your life?

_____

_____

_____

_____

What can you incorporate into your daily routine that will be additive?

_____

_____

_____

_____

Chapter 9

PRIORITIES

Whatever is on your plate got there because you said yes to it.

—*DANIELLE LAPORTE*

When my daughter, Jenna, was in first grade, she had a wonderful teacher named Mrs. Walsh. Mrs. Walsh styled her gray-blonde hair in a sensible bob and wore little makeup on her deeply lined skin. She favored crisp, button-down shirts with slacks, a silk scarf with a perfect knot covering her neck, and low-heeled pumps. She exuded the competence of a person who had worked hard to master her profession, and her life. Of all the options for the first grade at our neighborhood elementary school, Mrs. Walsh's class was the most coveted. She was dedicated to the kids, had a deep reserve of patience, and really made learning fun for them. When the PTA decided to nominate her for the Teacher of the Year award in our district of sixteen public schools, no one was surprised.

The Teacher of the Year competition required a significant amount of work on the part of the nominees. There was a lengthy submission process, including an application form, essays, and in-person interviews with the selection committee. There were administrative hoops to jump through as well. Mrs. Walsh looked at what was involved, and shortly thereafter she sent the PTA a letter declining the nomination.

In the letter she explained her decision to withdraw. She outlined her two highest priorities: her first priority was to be the best wife/mom/grandma she could be, and her second priority was to be the best teacher she could be. And as honored as she felt at being nominated, she'd regretfully decided not to go through with the application process because it was a major time commitment that wasn't aligned with either of her highest priorities. The truth as she saw it was, although the award would be a great honor, it wouldn't actually make her a better teacher.

I read Mrs. Walsh's letter with great interest and curiosity. Mrs. Walsh purposefully lived her life in alignment with her priorities. She consciously created that life with her decisions each day. And even when given the opportunity to be recognized for her accomplishments, she had the clarity of mind and discipline to say no and protect her time.

It was, to use the words of Oprah Winfrey, an "a-ha moment" for me.

I was a busy mompreneur with four kids and a husband. I had a house and a yard and a dog and a rabbit and three fish.

I made delicious meals, I volunteered in the kids' schools, and I kept my house relatively clean. That was the surface.

Underneath that surface-level success, I had a to-do list a mile long. The interior pages of my *momAgenda* were so packed each week with activities, scribbles, cross-outs, and rewrites, my crazed scrawlings might suggest to some I was deranged.

There were days when I barely had time to have a glass of water or to stop for a pee break. I said yes to everything that was asked of me, and as a result I ran around trying to get everything done. But there was no real criteria or selectivity in terms of what I agreed to do or where I put my energy. For example, I said yes to serving on a PTA committee simply because a friend asked me to do it. Saying no felt uncomfortable. I said yes to running the social committee in a women's group I belonged to, because the person who asked me boosted my ego by telling me I'd been chosen specifically because of my particular skills and talents (I found out later I was the fourth person who'd been asked to fill the role—the first three had declined).

In the midst of all the chaos and craziness of raising young children, I'd lost sight of my priorities and let my life spin out of control. My life was full but not in the way I wanted it to be. I wanted it to be filled with love and connection with my kids, with closeness and intimacy with my husband, with fun activities that had meaning for my family, with the fulfillment I got from building my business and watching it succeed.

Instead it was filled with errands and tasks and unfulfilling, pressured-into-accepting "must-dos."

I felt pressured, but in reality, no one had held me down and threatened to torture me if I refused to run the bake sale at the school fundraiser. I volunteered to do it and was angry with myself afterward. When I tried to reflect upon why I was addicted to yes, I realized that I held myself to this crazy standard that I had to do it all, I had to say yes to everything, because that's what good moms do. Not having time for basically everything was, in my mind, a sign of failure.

I was a child of the '70s. I remember the perfume commercial with the song lyrics, "I can bring home the bacon, fry it up in the pan, and never, never, never let you forget you're a man...'cause I'm a woman." I expected that I, too, would someday bring home the bacon (earn lots of money), fry it up in the pan (care for my family), and never forget my partner is a man (wasn't sure what that meant at the time, but it definitely sounded fun). This fragrance ad encapsulated the idea that being a modern woman meant not just having it all, but also *doing it all*. That cultural conditioning is deeply embedded in us, as the generation of women who were raised to do it all and look hot (and, apparently, smell good) doing it. We put these crazy expectations on ourselves to be supermoms because that's what we've been taught to do since we were young kids.

My preconceived notions of being a mom made Mrs. Walsh's seemingly radical decision intriguing to me. Here was a woman who was not seeking the superwoman cape. She didn't need to have it all. She didn't need to do it all. In fact, she only wanted to do two things, and she declined everything else. She'd decided to live her life on her terms, and she didn't need to gain the approval of her community in order to affirm she was doing a good job. She'd outlined her priorities and decided to live by them and, as a result, had total clarity about her decisions.

Inspired by Mrs. Walsh's letter to the PTA, I sat down at my desk, took out a Post-it note, and wrote the following:

1. Be a great mom

2. Build my business

I put the Post-it note inside the front cover of my *momAgenda*, where I'd see it every day. Each time I was presented with a new potential commitment, I asked myself, "Does this commitment help me be a great mom or build my business?"

When one of the kids' schools called and asked me to help out, I asked myself whether this volunteer commitment would help me be a great mom. If the commitment involved being in the classroom and actually interacting with my child, then the answer was yes. If not, the answer was no. When a new opportunity came up at work, I asked myself if that opportunity had the potential to grow the company. If the answer was yes, I took on the project. If the answer was no, I didn't.

I had set my priorities.

That year, when school ended and after summer, the new one began, I started a new *momAgenda*, and I transferred the Post-it note with it. I still have that little yellow Post-it note, although now it's looking very worn down from years of existence. For me, it represents the moment in my life when I finally gained control of my schedule, rather than allowing my schedule to control me.

Instead of Doing It All, Do Less. A Lot Less.

The beauty of setting priorities and living by them is you actually get to do less as a result. You streamline your activities and your life by only doing the things that are in alignment with who you are and what you want. You still do the things you want to do and live the life you want to live. You simply cut out all the tasks and responsibilities that aren't aligned with your priorities. *You only do what matters most to you.*

And it makes it so much easier to say no to people when you identify your priorities and make the decision that your activities will be aligned with them. You don't have to torture yourself or second-guess yourself about making a decision—it becomes easy and effortless. You gain the clarity to create the life you really want, starting with the decisions you make about what you're going to do with your time each day.

When we want to gain control over our schedules most of us look at our calendars and try to cut things. This is the *outside-in* approach. The problem with this approach is that it's not strategic and it won't get you any closer to your goals or the life you really want to live. You end up cutting out things that are easy to cut, rather than things that are less important to you. As a result, you end up with a schedule full of commitments that are hard to get out of and aren't particularly important to you.

In order to live the life you truly want, the life that truly reflects who you are and your values, be like Mrs. Walsh and start from the inside out. Ask yourself what you really want. Set your priorities based on your unique desires and see how your life starts to shift. If you can set aside your daily life and think big picture, your priorities will reflect the life you really want to live, not just what seems important in the short term.

Clarity through the Cloud of Overthinking and Emotional Thinking

Sometimes our emotions can cloud our thinking, and that's where prioritizing really comes in handy. If Mrs. Walsh were thinking emotionally, I imagine she might have made a different decision. In an alternate universe, it could have gone like this:

"Well, it was so nice of them to nominate me, and I don't want to hurt their feelings by declining, and if I decline they'll think I'm ungrateful, so I should probably say yes. Also, I may never be nominated for an award again, and it would be so cool to have that certificate to frame and hang on my wall, and for the rest of my life I'd know that everyone really thought I did a good job…"

This type of thinking is truly never ending. It is possible to justify any decision if you approach it emotionally. Your mind can play tricks on you and make anything seem okay in the moment. That is why you need to work hard to avoid overthinking and emotional thinking when you're evaluating your priorities.

Instead, I recommend *not thinking at all.* Use your gut instead. When you make your list of potential priorities, or any big decisions for that matter, rather than listening to your thoughts, pay attention to what feels right in your body. Your gut isn't in your mind, it's in your body, and your body knows what's most important to you.

According to research outlined by life coach extraordinaire Martha Beck, your brain processes information at forty bits of information per second. But your nervous system that runs through your body processes information at the rate of eleven million bits per second. Your body is infinitely smarter than your mind, and your body is sending messages to your mind all the time. So learn to listen to the wisdom of your body—it knows.

Your body speaks to you in feelings, so pay attention. When you look over your list of potential priorities, which make you feel light and expansive? Which make you feel excited? On the other hand, which make you feel contracted, closed off, or stressed? Which items give you a pit in your stomach or a sinking feeling? Paying attention to these signals from your body goes a long way toward uncovering the priorities that matter most to you.

It's All about You

A person's list of priorities is as unique as a fingerprint, and that's one of the reasons it's so important to identify yours—otherwise, you can get caught up in going with the flow of what everyone's doing in your community, rather than honoring your unique desires and needs.

Living your priorities means living in alignment with your deepest values. In knowing and articulating your priorities, you give yourself the gift of clarity in terms of what those values are. Understanding what you value most helps you understand yourself better and informs everything in your life, from big decisions to small ones.

Today's To-Dos: Make a Priority Worksheet

Make a list of the ten most important things in your life right now. It might include things like parenting, being a spouse/partner, working, exercising, managing your health, or being a good friend.

When setting your priorities, think long term. Think about what you really want, not just today or this year, but five to ten years from now and beyond. Do you want to write a book? Then add to the list: write for an hour each day. Do you want to be healthy and fit? Then add eating healthy and working out most days. Do you want the life partnership of your dreams? Write it down.

Now, go through that list and cross out five things that aren't your highest priorities. You should have five items left on your list.

It's challenging, but cross out two more things that aren't your *highest* priorities.

Now you know what your top three priorities are. Write those things down in your day planner—I like to put mine on a Post-it note inside the front cover of my *momAgenda*, so I can refer to them easily. Create a new Note in your phone and list the items there as well. I also recommend writing them down on Post-it notes and putting them on your desk, your fridge, your bathroom mirror, and anywhere else you need a reminder.

Every time you receive a request, consult your Post-it note. Make decisions every day going forward through that priority lens. Ask yourself if the request is aligned with the priorities you've identified. If it's not, say no without guilt or regret. If it is aligned and you have the time and bandwidth, say yes and enjoy.

Chapter 10

NO WAY, NO THANK YOU, AND OTHER COMPLETE SENTENCES

> *If you want to live an authentic, meaningful life,*
> *you need to master the art of disappointing and*
> *upsetting others, hurting feelings, and living with*
> *the reality that some people just won't like you.*
>
> —CHERYL RICHARDSON

My best friend smiled as she read the text message that had just come in. "Yes!" she shouted, startling me. "The bike trip is on!"

I put a fake smile on my face. "Awesome!"

My friend was almost childlike in her enthusiasm for the bike trip. I, on the other hand, had suddenly developed a sinking feeling in my gut. This was not good news for me. But I didn't want to be the Grinch that crushed her Christmas-morning-level excitement and anticipation for the weekend with friends.

Each year, a group of my friends organized a bike trip around Block Island, a quaint, New England island dotted with homes, shops, and quiet beaches, just a couple of hours away from home. Calling it a "bike trip" was a bit misleading, though, as it was really just a day-drinking expedition that happened to take place on Block Island. The bikes were merely the primary mode of transportation to various drinking locales. The year in question, the organizer had been too busy to book hotel rooms in advance, and Airbnb options on the tiny island are limited, so the plan was to bring tents and camp out on the beach.

I didn't want to camp. As a teenager, I once went on a week-long canoe trip with my group of about ten girlfriends. My friend Lindsay's uncle guided our trip. He was a professional guide with deep lines on his face from years of experience guiding youth groups on all manner of outdoor adventures. We loaded our gear into ancient wood-sided Jeep Wagoneers and made our way up the windy country roads into upstate New York. Then, once we reached our destination, we paired off into canoes, paddling for hours each day down the mostly peaceful river, and finding a new spot each evening to pitch our tents and camp out for the night.

At the end of the trip, we staged a little awards ceremony, where we celebrated the end of the trip and congratulated ourselves on our accomplishments from the week. One of my friends was voted Best on White Water, for her ability to keep her cool in the occasional rough waters we hit along the way.

My friend Laura was voted Best Attitude for how she courageously laughed off a mysterious bug bite on her lower lip that caused it to swell up to about five times its normal size, making her look like the Elephant Man with bleach-blonde beach waves.

My friends voted me Least Outdoorsy.

It's not that I had a bad time on the trip—I actually had fun. But the outdoors is not my natural habitat. When I go on vacation, I prefer to sleep on a bed in a temperature-controlled room and go out to dinner (or order room service). While that canoe trip was enjoyable, it was way outside my comfort zone. It was one of those things I was glad I did once, mostly so I'd never have to do it again.

When faced with the prospect of camping on Block Island, my overwhelming instinct was to say no. I didn't want to say no to the camping trip because I didn't want to be that person who says no. It felt like I was being difficult, and I was afraid everyone would like me less if I said no.

Additionally, I felt insecure about what my friends would think of me upon realizing I'm not the outdoorsy type. After all, doesn't everyone want to be outdoorsy? Isn't being outdoorsy a universally desirable quality, like being funny or smart or good-looking?

Still, I decided on an answer. No. The answer, at least for the camping portion of the bike trip, was no from me. I went on the bike trip for the day, caught the last ferry back to the mainland in the evening, and slept that night in a comfortable hotel room.

Overcoming overwhelm, setting priorities, and drawing boundaries are critically important for a happy life. We can have the best intentions, making lists and setting goals and scheduling our priorities all day long, but if we don't master the art of saying no, none of it is going to work.

That's why I'd like to introduce you to one of my favorite words in the English language. That word is *no*. Here's how to get good at no:

Greed Is Good

Remember that epic line from the movie *Wall Street*? *Greed is good*. Well, I agree, as it pertains to being greedy about protecting yourself and your time.

It wasn't always that way for me. I had to work at it. That's because I had an aversion to using the word *no*. It was all about avoiding the pain, the physical discomfort I felt. I was afraid people wouldn't like me, they'd think I was difficult, and they'd talk about me behind my back.

But that all changed once I got my priorities in check. This admission to my love of no may be shocking to you. What kind of person admits to loving the word no? Our society glorifies the word yes. We're taught yes indicates a positive, can-do attitude and a willingness to get things done. Yes suggests a mind and spirit that's open to new possibilities. In my first job out of college, one of the first pieces of advice I was given was to *say yes first, then figure it out later,* in order to show our demanding clients our ability to handle anything that happens. There have been bestselling books written about the power of yes, the year of yes, the yes attitude, and the yes brain.

We need no. Living your best possible life isn't just about letting the good stuff in. It's also about keeping the bad stuff, the stuff that's not aligned with your goals and priorities, the stuff that isn't right for you, out.

Sometimes saying yes is important, but it's not the only right answer. Our glorification of saying yes has done untold harm. By glorifying yes, we demonize no. We create an atmosphere in which no seems negative, harmful, limiting, and a hard stop. As a result, many of us aren't practiced in the art of saying no.

Simply put, you can't live a happy, healthy life until you master this important skill.

No is a protective shield in many ways. No is a simple mechanism that puts a safe boundary around you, often shielding you from negativity. No protects your relationships from resentments. No protects your time, keeping you from overcommitting yourself. No protects your body, keeping you from touching or being touched in ways you don't want to be. No keeps you healthy. No is a way of only letting in what's right for you, at the right time for you. No is, very often, a way of allowing you to honor your needs, your wants, your desires, and your best life.

Saying no to someone else is, very often, a way of saying yes to you.

It's simple to say no, but it's not necessarily easy. The ability to say no does not always come naturally to us as women. We don't want others to be critical of us or angry at us, and we want to avoid conflict. Many of us come to adulthood after years of being taught, as children, not to say no. We've been raised to be compliant and agreeable, to do as we're told, and to do everything in our power to be liked and accepted. Saying no feels unnatural because it goes against our programming, which was established when we were very young. For some people, saying no can cause uncomfortable symptoms of anxiety, such as dizziness and lightheadedness.

We've learned to communicate indirectly from our families of origin. We've learned not to say what we mean, because it might be considered mean. We've internalized what many of our parents taught us, that expressing feelings and opinions is wrong, that directly stating our needs is wrong, and that saying no is flat-out rude. Saying no was considered rude and unacceptable in my family of origin. Doing so could get me grounded, or worse.

Saying no is ultimately about *loving yourself.* It's about getting so comfortable with yourself that you're okay with whatever other people think of you. It's about trusting yourself, your feelings, and your opinions to be *right for you.*

Maybe they're not right for someone else, but they're right for you. It's about loving and liking yourself so much that you're willing tolerate others not liking you, your feelings, and your opinions. It's saying, "I love you, but I love me more."

Saying no is also about *knowing yourself*. Many women haven't done the important work of uncovering their unique needs and wants, and ridding themselves of the guilt sometimes associated with having their own lives. In order to say no with confidence, you need to have clarity on who you are, what your priorities and boundaries are, and what your wants and needs are. The steps you'll take in this book will help you gain that clarity.

You don't need to offer up an explanation when you say no, nor do you need to justify or rationalize your no. You also don't need to apologize. You don't need to soften it by saying, "I'm not sure," "Maybe," or "I don't think so." You don't need to justify your decision to anyone else. What other people think actually doesn't matter. As long as you say it nicely, you can say no to anything you want and hold your head high. It really doesn't matter why you're saying no, or why you're making excuses. Attempting to justify it only weakens your statement. Say it simply and directly, with kindness and respect, and with no added commentary or excuse-making. If you need some assistance, I've provided a few scripts at the end of this chapter.

Saying no is, ultimately, one of the most important tools for putting your needs back on the to-do list. By saying no to what's not right for you, you're creating space for what is right for you.

1. If It's Not a Hell Yes, It's a No

I don't know who originally wrote about this concept. It's been attributed to a few different people including James Altucher, Derek Sivers, and others.

This is an easy-to-remember, important rule for those of us who tend to overcommit, do too much, or have a hard time saying no (that is, all of us). And it can be applied to every area of life, from work to relationships to how we choose to spend our leisure time.

When deciding whether to take on a new commitment or responsibility, check in deeply with yourself. We all have a soft voice inside of us that tells us how we really feel and what's right for us. The trick is to get really quiet so we can hear what that voice is saying…and then listen to it. Follow the guidance of that inner voice. If you feel anything other than *hell yes, I really want to do that,* say no.

Your life is precious and short. Do you want to spend valuable time in your life doing things you feel lukewarm about? Or do you want to spend your time doing things you are passionate about, excited about, deeply invested in?

Everyone is so busy, stressed out, exhausted, and over-committed, because we feel pressured to say yes to everything. So unless it's a hell yes, say no.

2. Erase It or Embrace It

One way to look at your to-do list is through the lens of erase it or embrace it. Erasing it means you're crossing it off your list because you're not going to do it. This is for tasks that aren't that important, such as rearranging your sock drawer or folding all your underwear. Those are tasks that objectively do not need to be done. Hopefully you don't have them on your to-do list, but if you do, please erase them, or just cross them off your list, right now!

Erasing it is also for tasks that could potentially be done by someone else. I like to erase taking out the garbage by getting my sixteen-year-old son to do it. Sometimes a barter will be involved in erasing it: find someone who likes doing what you're trying to erase and trade tasks with them. My son would much rather take out the garbage than load the dishwasher. So I might say to him, I'll load the dishwasher every night if you'll take out the garbage every night.

Embracing it means you're choosing to do the task and you're deciding to have fun with it. How can you make mundane tasks more fun? I always blast loud music while I tackle major cleanup projects around my house. Another way to make tasks more fun is to make them easier. So, instead of going to the grocery store, make it easier by ordering from one of the online services. Instead of braving the crowds at the mall at holiday time, do your shopping online. I even found a service that delivers and picks up my Christmas tree each year. Now I embrace the task of buying a Christmas tree—all I have to do is pick one out, and they do all the hard work involved in getting it set up in my house and removing it after the holidays are over.

Either cross it off your list or welcome it with open arms, make it fun, and enjoy it. There's no in-between here. Your goal is to be happy every day—that means you're not taking on anything you can't do with joy. Make a commitment to erase it or embrace it.

3. The No Way List*

You know that sinking feeling you get when you answer the phone and it's a telemarketer, and now you're stuck having to come up with an excuse to politely (or not so politely) get off the phone? Or when you answer the door and it's someone raising money to help save the oceans?

The no way list is a simple method for eliminating those everyday annoyances.

It's one of my favorite methods for not only drawing boundaries but also saving time, energy, and sanity.

There are certain things in life we don't want to do but we sometimes or often have to do. Changing diapers, disciplining our kids, and taking out the garbage come to mind. But there are other things we may think we have to do, or think we "should" do, but we really don't have to do at all.

For example, you don't have to answer the phone simply because it's ringing. My phone rang earlier today while I was working on a marketing project for *momAgenda*. Why should I interrupt my train of thought in the middle of an important project simply because of someone else's timetable?

The answer is I shouldn't, and fortunately I don't have to. Answering the phone when I'm in the middle of work, or with my kids, or to an unknown number at any time of day, is on my no way list. I just don't do it.

The same goes for answering the door. Unless I'm expecting someone or I know a package is coming that I'll need to sign for, I don't answer it. I work from home, and my doorbell rings a few times a week. I nearly always ignore it. So far, there have been no negative consequences. If it's important, they'll come back.

The no way list is a powerful tool for drawing boundaries around your personal time and space. It's an easy method to protect you from time-sucking, soul-draining activities that don't serve your highest good. And it's so easy. Simply open up your journal and write No Way at the top of the page. Then start brainstorming.

The beauty of the no way list is in its simplicity. You don't have to agonize over making a decision or even spending time thinking about it. I've wasted so much time thinking *should I or shouldn't I* in various scenarios. The no way list makes it easy to make a quick decision with no decision-making or ruminating involved. It's a set of rules you make for yourself, with no apologies or exceptions.

Your criteria for deciding what goes on the no way list will be unique to you, but here are a few potential criteria to consider:

✧ Things you don't want to do

✧ Things that don't feel good to you

✧ Things that have no clear positive end benefit for you or your family

Not answering the phone and not answering the door are just a starting point.

Here are a few more ideas from my own personal no way list to get you started:

✧ No checking email other than three times per day: first thing in the morning, lunchtime, and at the end of the day.

✧ No social media scrolling beyond five minutes at a time.

✧ No going out more than two nights per week.

✧ No reading books if I'm not enjoying them beyond page 100 (I try to give every book a chance before I give up).

✧ No giving time to people in my life who lie to me or drain my energy.

✧ No taking on other people's stuff (problems, emotions, issues).

Now it's your turn. What's going to be on your no way list? I encourage you to brainstorm as many things as possible. You can always edit it later.

I hope that, like me, you come to find your no way list to be an invaluable method for setting boundaries and spending your time your way, every day.

*The concept of the no way list was adapted from an exercise by Cheryl Richardson, an amazing life coach and self-care superstar.

How to Say No to Almost Anything

Lots of us are afraid that if we say no, people will like us less. I've started saying no a lot, and you know what? I think it's true. *People do like me less.* But, I've realized that I can live with this, that it's actually more important to me to live an authentic life than it is to be liked by every single person in my town. There's a saying that goes, "Those who mind don't matter, and those who matter don't mind." The people who are my friends accept me and my boundaries. The people who aren't my friends don't matter. Why worry about those people?

This section is a cheat sheet, providing you with easy scripts to get out of situations you really don't want to get into. Saying no can be uncomfortable, so having a script can take the edge off this discomfort. Once you get into the habit of knowing when to say no and saying it respectfully and confidently, you'll start doing it without a script.

First, let's set some realistic guidelines around the implications of a yes—mainly, time. Sometimes when we're asked to take on a project, we want to please the other person so much that we talk ourselves into it. We rationalize that it won't take much time, and this leads us to underestimate the size of the project. I'm guilty of this as well. I've found that a good rule of thumb, when you're evaluating how much time a project will take, is to take your estimate and add 30 percent. So if you think it's going to take six hours, keep in mind that it's more realistically going to take eight hours. Knowing that, proceed accordingly.

Also remember that when you say no to a commitment that doesn't work for you, *you're actually doing the other person a favor*. If they're asking you to do something you don't fully want to participate in, you're doing them a favor by allowing them to find someone who's all in on that activity. So second thing to remember here: don't feel guilty about saying no! It's a win-win for everyone.

A Note about Saying It Nicely

There's a saying that goes, "Mean what you say and say what you mean, but don't say it mean." Saying it nicely is the trick to saying no effectively, without alienating anyone unintentionally. Usually, if we say it respectfully and considerately, we realize that all our fears about the person getting mad at us were unfounded. You simply want to suggest you're very busy, your schedule is already full, and it's nothing personal. People will understand this, because their calendar is probably very full as well.

I like to always be honest when saying no to someone (and all the time). It's easier to tell the truth, because then you never have to think about it again, and you never have to worry about being called out. In addition, I think people can usually sense when they're being lied to. Using some variation on the theme of "I'm too busy" has served me well over the years because, generally, it's true. It is the overarching reason why I don't take on many outside commitments, outside of work and my kids. I'm too busy with the priorities that are most important to my life.

Note that saying it nicely is not the same as making up excuses or offering explanations. You don't need to explain yourself or justify your decision. In fact, doing so may suggest to the other person that you're insecure about your decision. So don't try to explain your rationale for saying no in any sort of great detail. You simply need to treat other people with kindness and respect when saying no to them. Short and sweet is the strongest and most effective approach.

✧ It goes without saying that if someone invited you to go somewhere or do something, your no should always be preceded by a thank you. Thank you for inviting me, thanks for asking me, thanks for thinking of me, thanks for the note.

✧ Say it with a smile. That keeps your tone in positive territory.

✧ Try to tap into genuine gratitude for the other person when you say no. Keep in mind the person asking you to do something is not you, is not in the same place as you, and has no idea what's going on in your internal world. They don't know that you feel overwhelmed and stressed, because they're not you. So don't be angry at them for asking. Strip away any opinions about that person, other than holding genuine gratitude to them for considering you.

✧ Note that none of these scripts have the words *sorry* or *I apologize* in them. I don't believe you need to apologize for saying no. An apology implies you're doing something wrong, which you're not. You're choosing how to spend your time and, in doing so, how you live your life. You're choosing to be a person with healthy boundaries around your time. There's never an apology required for that.

Three Quick Steps to No

1. Say something positive. Here are a few ideas:

"Thank you for thinking of me!"

"It's awesome that you've taken on the PTA presidency this year!"

"This sounds like an interesting project, and I'm flattered that you thought of me!"

"A book club sounds fun, and it sounds like you've put together an amazing group!"

2. Now, just do it. Say no. Keep it as brief as possible, like this:

"My plate is so full right now, so I have to say no this time."

"I'm not taking on any new projects/responsibilities/clubs right now, so unfortunately I have to decline."

"My calendar is already packed, so I can't commit to that right now."

"The timing isn't right for me right now, so I have to say no, unfortunately."

3. Finally, offer up another positive:

"If my calendar clears up in the near future I will definitely reach out to you!"

"Thanks again for reaching out!"

"Enjoy your weekend!"

A Scenario-by-Scenario Script to No

How to say no to plans you don't want to participate in

- ✧ "Thanks for inviting me! I'm going to pass on this one, but please keep me posted on future plans!"

- ✧ "Thanks for thinking of me! At the moment I'm so swamped, I'm not putting anything new on the calendar. Maybe next time!"

How to say no to lunch/drinks/dinner

- ✧ "That sounds fun—thanks for thinking of me! I'm slammed for the next few weeks, but let's get together when things calm down for both of us."

- ✧ "I'd love to see you and hang out! Unfortunately, I'm crazed and can't lock anything in right now, but let's get back in touch when things are less hectic. Thanks for checking in."

How to say no to joining a book club or other group

- ✧ "Sounds fun! Thanks for inviting me. I'm trying to scale back on my commitments, so I have to say no for right now, but I'll let you know if anything changes."

- ✧ "What an awesome idea, thanks for including me. My time is super limited right now so I have to say no, but thank you again for thinking of me, and enjoy!"

How to say no to taking on a new project (for example, a new PTA role or joining the class gift committee at your alma mater)

✧ "Thanks for asking! It sounds like a fun project, but I'm already overbooked with commitments for this school year. Best of luck with it."

✧ "I'd love to help, but I'm not able to put much more on my plate at this time, unfortunately. Thanks for thinking of me!"

✧ "Thanks for thinking of me! I'm currently swamped with [my job, my book, my kids, college applications], so I don't have the bandwidth to take on anything new at this time. But I'll make a small financial contribution so I can continue to support my wonderful alma mater."

How to say no to making a financial contribution

✧ "What an amazing cause! I've already blown past my donation budget for the year, so I can't make a contribution at this time. But thanks for reaching out, and I wish you all the best on reaching your goal."

How to say no to someone who wants to meet with you for work

✧ "Thanks for getting in touch! My time is extremely limited right now so I'm not setting up any new meetings, but I'll let you know if/when that changes."

✧ "Thanks for thinking of me! I'd love to meet with you, but the timing isn't great for me at the moment. Keep me posted on your progress, please!"

How to buy time when you want to say no but aren't 100 percent sure
✧ "Thanks for thinking of me! I need a little bit of time to think about whether I can commit to this. Can I get back to you in a few days? Thanks again!"

Saying no becomes easier with practice. When it's done with kindness and respect, and out of our own genuine need to assert personal boundaries, it's liberating. It feels good to look at your calendar and realize that everything on your list, everything you've committed to, is something you've chosen because of your needs, your desires, your priorities, and your boundaries. You realize you've gained the clarity to say yes to what works for you, and no to what doesn't, without regret or second-guessing.

Today's To-Dos: Embracing No

In your journal, practice saying no by writing your own scripts, in your own words, for various scenarios that you frequently or occasionally face. Try a script for saying no to lunch plans, saying no to a networking cocktail party, saying no to a post on the PTA board, and saying no to joining a group or club.

Chapter 11

SECRET WEAPONS

All there is to do, right at this very moment, is to breathe in, breathe out, and kiss the joy as it flies.

—DANI SHAPIRO

Andrew got into the car and let his backpack drop to the floor. He slammed the car door shut. "I hate everyone," he muttered. Translation: *I'm in a shitty mood, and there's nothing you or anyone else can do to make me happy right now.*

"What happened?" I asked, though I suspected I already knew the answer.

He'd taken a test that day, and I also knew he'd had an audition for the school musical. My heart sank for him. He was a junior in high school, and his grades and theater were all that really mattered to him, not just because of his self-image, but because of his college transcript.

"My teacher is so stupid," he said. "None of the stuff she told us to study for was on the test. There goes my A average in that class. And on my transcript. I can basically forget about college."

Andrew, I should mention, was prone to catastrophizing.

"You always do better than you think you did on tests," I reminded him.

We'd had this conversation hundreds of times over the years, and no matter how convinced he was of his failings, he always did well in school.

He ignored me and continued with his diatribe. "Then I had my audition, and it was a disaster," he said. "Disaster! My voice sounded so bad. The choreography was totally confusing, and I couldn't get the dance moves. I'll be lucky if I get a part in the chorus." Andrew was confident in his acting skills but less so in his singing and dancing.

"The chorus is stupid!" he went on. "I'll be invisible. There's no point. It's ridiculous. There's no reason to be in the musical if I'm in the chorus. I should just quit theater. I'm not that good, and I don't know why I even try." Catastrophizing again. His anxiety, always a concern of mine, was spiraling out of control.

I tried talking him through his various issues. He tended to assume the worst, but his grades were excellent. And despite several self-described "bad" auditions, he'd gotten a significant role in every play he tried out for.

He shook his head and rolled his eyes, disagreeing with me. Apparently, I was stupid too. I knew there was nothing

I could say. He was stuck, as though he'd fallen into a hole and couldn't claw his way out. He'd always been that way, a kid who had a hard time finding his own way out of his own difficult feelings.

When Andrew was a baby, he cried and cried. I still don't know, to this day, if his stomach hurt or his teeth hurt or what was really wrong with him. At the time I tried everything I could think of to soothe him. His response to the pacifier was to throw it across the room. Distraction with a book or a toy was futile.

One day while cooking dinner, I picked him up and held him, nearly crying myself from frustration and lack of sleep and the sadness I felt at not being able to soothe my child. Mariah Carey happened to be on the radio. Coincidentally, the song was called "Always Be My Baby." As I bounced him gently along to the music, "Do do do, do…do do do, do do, do do…," I noticed that he was starting to calm down. I danced a little bit, swaying him back and forth. Still sniffling, he rubbed his eyes with his chubby little hand.

After just a minute or so his crying stopped, and he rested his head on my chest, his eyes getting heavy. I kept bouncing and swaying, just letting myself move gently to the song. Soon he was sound asleep.

After that, music became my go-to when Andrew became inconsolable. He responded well to Mariah Carey, so I bought the latest CD and started playing it in the house. All I had to do was pick him up and start dancing with him to the music, and he'd calm down almost immediately. Sometimes he'd even fall asleep.

And so it began. Andrew's secret weapon is music. Studying musical theater had helped to expand his repertoire beyond Mariah Carey hits, and eventually he grew to favor classic Broadway show tunes.

That day as he was on his tear about his terrible audition, I pulled the car over, took my iPhone out of my bag, and found a playlist on Spotify. I scrolled through until I found what I was looking for. I made sure my Bluetooth was connected and hit play. Soon the music filled our car, and Kelly Clarkson belted it out like Ethel Merman on steroids.

I looked at Andrew and smiled. His whole face softened as he let his head relax against the headrest, closed his eyes, and let the song fill up his body. He knew exactly what I was doing, and, best of all, he let it work.

By the end of the song his mood had transformed. He created a catastrophe when he felt vulnerable or uncertain, but it was self-created, all in his head, and not related to the reality of what was true in his life. All he needed was a quick hit of his secret weapon to get out of his head and into a mental space where he could think rationally again.

(And by the way, Andrew got a leading role in that show and aced the test that day.)

Secret Weapons Explained

We can practice being strategic about our self-care, but sometimes life gets in the way and we get stuck. When our usual methods fail, secret weapons are there as a backup. For baby Andrew, that Mariah Carey song was a secret weapon. What is a secret weapon? It's a tool we can use to practice quick, effective self-care, anytime, anywhere.

Think of a baby who cries when she's uncomfortable. What do you do to soothe her? Each baby is different, but most parents know which methods work with each child to stop the tears. You, too, can soothe yourself when you're uncomfortable, or anxious, or sad, or away from home, or just in need of a boost. You need not be crying like a six-month-old to use your secret weapon. Like Andrew's show tunes, it makes you feel good no matter where you are or what you're doing.

There are as many ways to soothe ourselves as there are people on this planet. As an introvert, I favor methods that tend to be more calming and inward-focused. Yours might be more outward-focused, such as going out to a party. You might love the distraction of a true crime podcast. There's no right or wrong when it comes to secret weapons. It's all about what works for you, what helps you flip the switch when you're not feeling your best.

These are a few of my favorite secret weapons, but please don't limit yourself to this list:

1. Breathe

It seems so simple, but breathing is one of the best secret weapons that exists. I'm talking about conscious breathing, with focused attention on the inhale and exhale. Focusing on breathing in and out does wonders for your mind and provides near-instant calm. When you're feeling calm, you can respond, rather than react, to whatever external circumstances are occurring.

2. Use Affirmations

Giving yourself peace of mind can be as easy as taking control of your thoughts. Using a positive affirmation can be helpful in anchoring your thoughts when your mind is like a runaway train, going full speed in the wrong direction. Over time, if you repeat an affirmation often enough, your subconscious mind will actually start to believe it. In this way, you can begin to create the reality you wish to have in your life.

Using an affirmation is easy. You simply need to commit to it. Write it on a Post-it note or on a note on your phone, or in your day planner, and repeat it to yourself regularly throughout the day. You'll quickly start to feel the benefits of this simple practice.

Here are a few affirmations I like and use regularly in my life:

Only good things are happening in my life.

Everything is working out perfectly.

I love, accept, and approve of myself.

I have more than enough time to do everything I choose to do.

I am more than enough.

I am perfectly healthy in mind, body, and spirit.

All my needs are met with ease.

I am grateful for the abundance in my life.

I trust my intuition to guide me at all times.

I breathe and relax knowing the universe supports me.

I am powerful and strong.

3. Listen to Music

"Without music, life would be a mistake," said Nietzsche, confirming my own deep suspicion.

I have Spotify playlists designed for every mood. The most important one, by far, is my recovery playlist. That's the one I listen to when I'm feeling down or heartbroken or just in need of a boost. The songs are upbeat and catchy takes on girl power, lots of Madonna and Britney and Beyonce. Music is one of my favorite secret weapons because it has the ability to change my mood almost instantaneously.

It turns out that there's scientific evidence that supports my theory that music has the ability to improve mood despite trying external circumstances. The reason: music causes the brain to release dopamine, a chemical that causes our bodies to be flooded with good feelings. Dopamine is also released during sex, or when eating, taking drugs, and gambling, among other activities. It's a feel-good drug that comes from deep within your own body. We're wired to derive intense pleasure and good feelings from music, as evidenced by the fact that music has held an important place in cultures worldwide, since the dawn of history.

Don't deprive yourself of this important source of pleasure. Make yourself a playlist that moves you so this secret weapon is always ready when you need it.

4. Move Your Body

Moving your body is one of the most surefire secret weapons in your arsenal. And you can tap into it no matter who you are. Studies show that when you move your body and get your blood flowing, you feel good. That's because moving your body causes your brain to produce endorphins. Endorphins, also known as "nature's painkillers," cause you to feel euphoric and combat feelings of stress. Endorphins are the reason we feel clearheaded and happy after even just twenty minutes of walking or running.

Even dancing will improve your mood. Studies have shown that dancing even for just five minutes elevates happiness levels. Dancing activates our pleasure centers to make us feel good instantaneously. Dancing can also provide an emotional release, a cathartic letting go of emotions that are pent-up in the body. It can release as happiness, or for some people, it can make them cry. When dancing is done purely for pleasure, not for performance, it can be a powerful means of accessing your deeper emotions and expressing them.

So, when you have a moment of feeling down, try moving your body for a few minutes. Science says your mood will improve significantly as a result.

5. Get Outside

Getting outside and spending time in nature, also known in some cultures as "forest bathing," is another instant secret weapon, lowering our stress levels and increasing our happiness levels almost instantaneously. We intuitively know that being out in nature makes us happy, but why?

Studies show that being outside in natural environments lowers cortisol levels, which are a key marker of stress, and that walks in nature are associated with lower rates of depression and anxiety. In addition, natural daylight helps raise your serotonin levels (feel-good chemicals), helping you naturally achieve a more positive mood. Getting outside for ten to twenty minutes a day can also help boost your memory and your immune function, so there are many reasons to make this one of your primary secret weapons.

6. Get Cozy

Put things on your body that are soft, warm, and scrumptious, that make you feel pampered. My kids gave me an oversized, chunky knit cardigan sweater that I've put on nearly every day after work for the last fifteen years. Even the softest cotton pajamas or sweatpants imaginable will work. Don't settle for kinda soft…wait till you find the ones that are so soft, that make you feel so bathed in comfort, that you feel compelled to put them on every day.

One of my favorite perks of attending trade shows is shopping for beautiful treasures. Even when the show is for the trade only, vendors are often willing to sell the samples from their booth at the end of the show. At one of the first trade shows I attended, I found a charcoal-gray cashmere blanket while visiting an Italian vendor who barely spoke any English. He took the folded blanket off the shelf, shook it open, and gently placed it around my shoulders. Oversized, the softness enveloped my entire body. I immediately felt calmer, seduced by the thick, rich feel of it. I envisioned days spent at the office, nights on my family room couch surrounded by family, and long plane rides wrapped up in the most delicious cashmere imaginable.

Needless to say, I negotiated the purchase and quickly became the proud owner of that blanket, and soon afterward it found a home draped over the back of the desk chair in my office. Every day after I dropped off the kids at school, I'd sit in my chair with my coffee, wrap my blanket around my shoulders, open up my laptop, and start my day. It didn't matter what the temperature was. The blanket made me feel safe and comfortable and cozy.

I don't like flying. So I always bring my cashmere blanket on the plane. It's one of several secret weapons that makes the experience tolerable for me. If you ever run into me on a plane, I guarantee the blanket will be wrapped around my shoulders or draped over my legs, making me feel warm and safe and cozy. I actually invested in an enormous new tote for traveling, to ensure my blanket will fit no matter what.

Last year, while my daughter, Jenna, was packing for an abroad study program three thousand miles from home, she asked if she could take my gray cashmere blanket. At first, I hesitated. I didn't want to part with it! Nearly fifteen years after I found it at the trade show, that blanket is still my portable safe haven, and my most cherished secret weapon. But then I thought of how terrified Jenna must have been feeling at the prospect of traveling away from her family and friends to live all alone in a strange country. The blanket would provide her with the comfort and security she needed, as well as a reminder of home.

I loaned her my blanket, first eliciting her promise to return it in one piece. And then, when Christmas rolled around, I bought her her very own blanket. Now that Jenna knows the importance of secret weapons, she'll never be without her own.

Today's To-Dos: Secret Weapon

What are your secret weapons? Write them down in your journal. Keep a running list. Think about experiences and things that bring you positive feelings, feelings of comfort, safety, security, happiness, satisfaction, and contentment. Be specific: Don't just say, "Go outside." Say, "Go for a walk at the beach with one of my BFFs."

What are your favorite affirmations? Make a list in your journal of the affirmations in this chapter that resonate for you. Then add a few more of your own. You can use Google to search for more, or you can make them up yourself! Just make sure they're easy to remember and that they resonate for you.

Chapter 12

SELF-CARE WHEN EVERYTHING SUCKS

She said to go ahead and feel the feelings. I did.
They felt like shit.

—ANNE LAMOTT

In a ball on the floor of the studio, I felt the first plaintive notes of the song. I didn't want to move, but my body involuntarily started to unfurl itself. Vertebra by vertebra, my spine uncurled, my arms uncrossed, and my head untucked. I opened my eyes. The studio was dark except for the light shining above the chair, where my dance-class friend sat, gazing down at me.

I couldn't meet her eyes, so I turned. My pain was too private at that moment. I managed to stand, and place my hands on my body, letting my hips circle. I felt the music move into my body as I did so, as though the music was pushing me, making me move.

My grief overcame me as my body moved and tears started flowing down my face. I wiped them away, determined to dance through my pain. I made my way across the room, where another chair sat empty. I let myself fall to my knees, my head on the ground, where my tears could flow in private. I kept moving through the music, the notes pushing me through my pain.

I felt another presence. I let my eyes open halfway, and in the dark of the studio I realized that my two teachers were with me. Cat behind me, Erin in front of me, they were moving with me. And although they weren't touching me, it felt like they were energetically holding me as I struggled to keep going. As I let their energy envelop me, the tears rushed out freely. I lost control; I simply let my body feel the loss and rage and sadness.

I knew in that moment that my life would never be the same.

In 2012, Larry and I decided to get a divorce. In my quest to be fully and authentically me, I'd finally let myself see the uncomfortable truth that my marriage to Larry had not been working. Our marriage had been over for years, but I'd kept this fact hidden from myself because it was too difficult and too complicated to face. When I finally decided to live in my truth, it was inescapable. My unhappiness was directly tied to cultural factors that I bought into that messed with my head—and with my relationship.

But getting divorced, even amicably as we did, put me through a sort of emotional pain I've rarely experienced in my life. And it's not solely because divorce is such a uniquely difficult experience, involving the unraveling of a complicated web that took seventeen years to weave, as well as the happiness and well-being of four children whom we both adore. It's also because, in my commitment to live fully in my truth, I'd decided that rather than run away from the pain, I was going to allow myself to feel it.

Cultural anthropologist Margaret Mead, when asked about her three failed marriages, replied, "What failure? I had three successful marriages for three different developmental periods of my life."

Each of her marriages was successful, she said, then came to a natural end. Sometimes we can go through our developmental phases with the same person, but as I learned (and I'm not saying it was easy) there's no shame in admitting when a relationship has run its course.

All these years later, with the messiness of a divorce over and the agony of going through it behind me, I have nothing but tremendous gratitude toward Larry. He's an amazing dad to our kids and a strong force for goodness and stability in their lives. He and his wife, Tara, are dear friends to me. And that's the truth of our relationship. Larry and I are friends, co-parents, and partners. Our relationship and our love for each other, now that we don't live together and are no longer married, are stronger and more beautiful than they've ever been. The relationship we have is the one we're meant to have at this stage of our lives. It took a lot of work for me to arrive at that truth, but self-care during and in the wake of it certainly helped.

Go through the Pain

Divorce or heartbreak, the death of a loved one, illness, and a crisis with one of the kids are all emotionally challenging, as are events that aren't tinged with loss and unhappiness, like a move or a new job. Life changes cause anxiety. Anxiety makes us want to curl up into the fetal position, hide under the covers, and avoid doing anything, or talking to anyone, never mind taking care of ourselves.

Two things can happen with anxiety—we withdraw from the world, or we do the opposite and fill our lives with activities, so we are distracted enough to feel nothing. Distraction comes in many forms. We eat too much. We escape into alcohol, or shopping, or exercise, or sugar binging, or social media scrolling, or mindless Netflix-watching. Or we throw ourselves into parenting or work or some other activity that keeps our mind occupied 24/7.

I call these activities *escape routes,* because they're easy escapes from the realities of life we'd rather not face. We choose these escape routes because they numb our pain and because we're afraid if we don't numb our pain, we may never stop hurting. The problem is that the numbing effect is temporary and does nothing to address the underlying issue that is causing the painful feeling. Numbing isn't self-care. It's the opposite.

The problem is anger, sadness, resentment, and other negative emotions require healthy processing. These feelings don't just go away with food. When not fully felt and experienced, these emotions linger under the surface and then eventually reemerge, often manifesting themselves in mental issues such as anxiety and depression, or in physical symptoms like headaches, back problems, and stomach issues. Compulsive busyness is just another way to mask the anxiety associated with facing the feelings that may result if you slow down and sit still for a moment.

I learned an important lesson during my divorce. Although we had the most amicable of divorces, it was still incredibly painful and destabilizing, and at one point I thought I might never stop crying. I was raised to always put a smile on my face and act like everything was "fine," no matter what the circumstance or how much pain I was in.

But Sherry reminded me of the words of a children's song I used to sing with my own kids. Do you remember *We're Going on a Bear Hunt?*

We can't go over it.

We can't go under it.

Oh no! We've got to go through it!

The most effective way to get through pain, and actually put it behind you, is to *go through it.*

What does going through it look like? It looks like leaning into the pain and *allowing yourself to fall apart.* It means accessing the part of you that's in pain and giving yourself permission to feel that pain. You can do that by sitting quietly, locating the place in your body where the pain is lodged (hint: it's often in the middle of your chest), and really feeling and noticing it until it starts to dissipate.

If a feeling comes, feel it. The pain is the long wavy grass, and the only way to put that long wavy grass behind you is to move forward, feeling the blades under your feet, maybe getting bugs on your face, feeling every bit of discomfort until that long wavy grass is far behind you in the distance.

Part of the problem, and the reason we try not to go through it but rather walk around it, is that we're not allowed to fall apart in our society. Many of us were raised to keep it together, no matter what's happening, to put a smile on our faces and act like *we've got this.* It makes others so uncomfortable to see us suffering, that they often give us advice that ironically makes the suffering last longer! Our parents teach us to "handle it," "get it together," or they dismiss our pain, saying, "You're fine."

As a result of this conditioning from our families, we grow up to be adults who believe that getting through a crisis means getting it together, putting on lipstick, and putting on a brave face for the world. Fact: we have been doing it completely backward! Forget about the brave face and the lipstick. Fall apart, cry, scream, punch things, and do whatever you can do to honor the pain you're feeling.

It takes courage to feel your own pain. It's a lot easier to stuff the pain down and pretend it's not there. But by choosing to face it, by showing up and feeling it, you're opening yourself up to learning the lessons that are contained in this particular heartbreak.

A study conducted at University of California, Berkeley, analyzed whether people feel their feelings or push them away, and the impact of either choice. The study found that people who tended to push away their feelings were less happy, and the people who accepted their feelings were, overall, less depressed and had a greater sense of well-being.

Follow these steps to learn how to feel your feelings, because reminder: *your needs matter.*

Step 1: When an unpleasant feeling comes, notice whatever thoughts arise ("I'll never find love," or "I'm messing up my kids' lives," or "My thighs are enormous"). As quickly as those feel-ings drifted into your mind, let them drift out. Let them go. Redirect your attention to your body. Where do you feel the unpleasantness? Try to locate the bad feeling in your body, being careful to continue to let go of any thoughts that arise.

Step 2: Stay with the physical sensations that are in your body. Experience those sensations. Notice the physical qualities of those sensations, such as heaviness in your chest or tightness in your shoulders. Notice where the sensations sit in your body. Your mind will want to add thoughts to this narrative, maybe to judge it or give it some meaning, but continue to redirect your focus back to simply noticing and experiencing the feeling in your body.

Step 3: Keep noticing the feeling in your body, treating it with gentleness and kindness, and refraining from judgment, until it slowly starts to dissolve. This usually only takes a couple of minutes.

Step 4: Repeat whenever an unpleasant thought arises.

As you go through the day, occasionally ask yourself, "How can I take care of myself in this moment?"

Lovingly detach from whatever situation you're dealing with and consider your own needs, beyond the needs of anyone else. Maybe you need fresh air or a cup of tea or an hour with a good book. Maybe you need to vent your frustrations at a boxing class or sweat through a hot yoga class.

This is advanced self-care—being there for yourself, having your own back, when times are difficult.

Life Happens for You, Not to You

When I was twenty-three, the man who I thought would someday be my husband ended our four-year relationship. It was my first major heartbreak, and I was initially devastated. I thought I'd never stop crying. After a few weeks, I started to venture out of my apartment again. My mom gave me extra money so I could join a gym, and I started exercising after work each day. I lost ten pounds, and all of a sudden I felt amazing in my body—I felt fit and like I looked good in my clothes, for the first time in ages. That gave me the confidence to start going out at night with my friends and actually have fun. I started flirting and enjoying life as a single woman. One day, a few months after my devastating breakup, it occurred to me that I was *thriving* post-breakup. Looking back on my past relationship, I realized I was happier without this man in my life than I'd been with him. When we were together, we'd fought constantly. It became clear, with distance, that I wanted more from our relationship than he was willing or able to give. And I wanted a deeper commitment than he was ready for. I'd been so carried away with the dream (the fantasy, really) of marriage and kids with this man that I'd lost sight of the reality of our relationship, which was that it wasn't making me happy.

Looking back, I'm so grateful to this man for ending a relationship that wasn't working. In addition, I'm grateful I didn't fight to hold on to that old relationship, which was clearly over. About a year after this heartbreak, I met Larry. Rather than looking at my past breakup as a devastating loss, I look at it as something old moving out of the way to make room for something new and even better.

The truth is, my breakups have been some of my greatest teachers. The most important lessons I've learned about myself and about life have come as a direct result of heartbreak and loss. At one time in my life I ran from the pain of loss, refused to grieve, and missed out on the lessons (and also created a lot of anxiety from all the repressed emotions trapped in my body). Now that I'm aware of the incredible lessons that come with loss, I've learned to let myself fall apart, feel the feelings, and grieve when I'm in the throes of heartbreak. It's only when you go through the pain, really feeling and experiencing every aspect of it, that you can come out on the other side with the beautiful new nuggets of wisdom that only great loss can deliver.

With that in mind, consider the positive outcomes that have resulted from your past crises or crappy situations. If you're able to reframe your experiences as things that are happening for you, rather than to you, it's easier to face the inevitable hardships that occur.

Crisis Management Self-Care

Self-care is challenging enough on regular days. Throw in motherhood, and it gets harder. But suddenly adding a crumbling marriage to the mix—forget it.

When you're deep in a crisis, with no end in sight, it's hard to know what's best for you. And there is no higher form of self-care than showing up for yourself.

Here are some things to try:

1. Take Your Hands off the Wheel

Taking your hands off the wheel, letting go of control and allowing life to unfold, can be surprisingly liberating. We try to control our days and our lives, and often we're able to maintain the illusion that life is totally within our control. We want to avoid bad outcomes that are sadly unavoidable. Unfortunately, things happen in life that we cannot plan for and would not have chosen for ourselves. The truth is, we have no control over other people or events that occur. The only thing we have control over is ourselves and our reaction to what happens. And we can choose to see what happens as a path to our highest good.

2. Call In Support

A couple of months after a crisis in my life, I booked consultations with no less than nine (not a typo) different mental health support providers (thankfully, over time I made choices and reduced that number significantly). They included psychiatrists, psychologists, life coaches, and of course my favorite acupuncturist. Those paid professionals were in addition to the dear friends who took me to dinner on a weekly basis and listened to me vent, and the loving family members who called each day to check in on me. There was never a day I felt unsupported or alone.

We talked in an earlier chapter about the importance of asking for help, but it's never more important than during a crisis. I can't stress this enough: what we need most during times of crisis is connection with others, not isolation. Please don't try to get through this yourself. Surround yourself with your tribe, and let them be there for you. When you're struggling, it's not only okay, it's imperative that you reach out to others for help.

3. Say Yes

I realize that for most of this book, we've focused on learning how to say no. But sometimes, we have to say yes. What I'm referring to here is surrendering to what is. Say yes to what's happening in your life, rather than fighting it by staying in denial. Fighting it just postpones the feelings.

I read somewhere that denial is the shock absorber for the soul. When something happens that's painful, we go into denial until we're ready to feel and process whatever it is that's happened. In that respect, denial is important. It gives us the gift of time that allows us to be ready to accept the truth of whatever reality we're facing. But we can't stay in denial, at some point it's necessary and healthy to move out of denial and into acceptance.

Fighting the truth doesn't make it less true. Denying it doesn't either. Throw up your hands and accept whatever it is that's happening. Say yes to it. Surrender to what is, rather than fighting and resisting. There's a reason this experience is coming into your life at this time, and the sooner you accept that, the sooner you'll move to the other side of your pain.

4. Journal

Sometimes, I honestly don't know how I feel about a given situation until I start writing about it in my journal. Then gradually, the truth spills out onto the page. Those of us who tend to respond emotionally can especially benefit from journaling, as it helps us gain clarity when our thoughts are clouded by emotion. Sometimes I go back and read what I wrote in the past and congratulate myself on how far I've come in my own journey.

5. Meditate

If there's one practice that I recommend above all others, it's meditation. I've been meditating for years and, despite the "woo-woo" connotation people often associate with it, there are real, concrete benefits such as:

✧ Reduced stress

✧ Reduced anxiety

✧ More positive feelings, reduced depression

✧ Improved sleep

This is not just anecdotal. There's hard scientific data that supports the idea that meditation measurably elevates your mood, reduces stress and anxiety, and helps you sleep better, plus a host of other benefits.

In addition to the measurable results, there are also intangible benefits to meditation. If you're a spiritual person, you can't help but notice a stronger connection to your intuition as a result of your meditation practice. You can call it your Higher Power of Source Energy or God…I call it my intuition. I find that meditation gives me a direct line to that innate wisdom.

I meditate for thirty minutes each day: fifteen minutes in the morning, before I start my day, and fifteen minutes in the late afternoon, just before dinner. When I first started meditation I viewed it as just another thing on my to-do list, but now I've come to look forward to my meditation sessions because it feels good and it gives me the support I need.

Today's To-Dos: When Everything Sucks
Practice feeling your feelings. Make a list and note what you're feeling in the moment. Don't censor yourself. Make a new list in a few hours and note how your feelings have changed. Practice doing this a few times per day until you start to notice your feelings naturally.

Make a list of a few things that have happened that have been painful for you (a breakup, a job loss, the loss of someone you love). Next, make a few bullet points under each "negative" experience. Each bullet point should be something positive that's happened as a result of the loss. For example, I wouldn't have been single and available when I met Larry if my previous boyfriend hadn't dumped me and broken my heart. As a result of that awful breakup, I found my future spouse and had four amazing kids with him.

Chapter 13
THE PURSUIT
OF HAPPINESS

*I have met myself and I am going to care for
her fiercely.*

—GLENNON DOYLE MELTON

Jenna came home from her therapy session and dropped her backpack on the kitchen countertop.

"How was it?" I asked her.

"Pretty good," she replied. "We talked about happiness."

Jenna, in high school at the time, had been seeing a therapist for about a year, ever since one of her closest friends was killed in a tragic accident.

"So, what did you learn about happiness?" I asked her, curious.

"I learned," she replied, "that I need to be *fiercely protective of my happiness.*"

I stopped what I was doing, moved by my daughter's words. "It's on me," she continued. "It's my responsibility to take care of myself, my feelings and my body, and my relationships. To make choices that make me happy in the long term. By doing that, it's like I'm putting a force field around myself that helps me protect my happiness."

I thought back to Jenna as a little girl, the most exuberant, charismatic, spirited child I've ever seen, her energy always high, her personality sparkling and dazzling everyone she met. The accident had taken so much from her. I was grateful to her therapist for teaching her how to begin to take it back, slowly and with baby steps. To help get her back to who she really was, her authentic, true self. To be fiercely protective of her happiness.

Prioritize Happiness

Some of us think we'll be happy once we acquire certain external things such as wealth or love. *If I only get that raise,* we think, *then I'll be happy!* The problem with this thinking is it always has us striving for more. We get a raise, but not a promotion. So we're happy about the raise briefly; then we're focused on getting the promotion. Or we find a relationship, but we decide what we *really* need is a deeper commitment—marriage or shared real estate. Then once we've accomplished that, we decide we won't really be happy until we have kids.

There's always another rung on the ladder when your happiness depends on external circumstances.

The truth is that long-term happiness has nothing to do with external things like making money or finding a relationship. Those rungs on the ladder can certainly give us a temporary boost, but we return to our normal happiness level pretty quickly. Studies have shown that even when people win the lottery, they experience a brief boost in happiness and then return to their previous level within about two years. Positive things happen, but even positive things we've been working toward our entire lives will eventually become the new normal.

One of the most important concepts I've learned about happiness is that it comes from within. Happiness comes from our own attitudes, our own mental states. It doesn't magically arrive when we get what we want. Choosing to be happy empowers us to create the life we want to live.

Your circumstances (for example, finally getting the job you want or the husband you want or the baby you want) are not what determines your happiness. It's actually the reverse.

When you choose to be happy, you choose to let go of negativity and destructive thought patterns. As a result, you're better able to connect with friends and family. You exercise and get outside more. You try new things, expanding your worldview. You take better care of yourself. You feel more motivated at work. Happiness empowers you to do things that lead to more happiness. So if you want to prioritize happiness, start by choosing to be happy every day.

I'm not saying it's easy. I'm saying it's a simple choice that we each get to make every single day.

Finding Your Tribe

Jerry Seinfeld once said in an interview about seeing his fellow comedy writers go onstage at the Emmy Awards to receive their prize: "You see these gnome-like cretins, just kind of all misshapen. And I go, 'This is me. This is who I am. That's my group.'"

A sense of connection is vital to our happiness, but it's not just connection with family that matters. We need to feel a sense of belonging, a sense of being welcomed and approved of, and that's where the modern-day "tribe" comes in.

It doesn't matter what they look like or if they're the cool group. They are the people with whom your soul is at home. Those are your people.

Find them. Find the people who make you feel like you can be yourself, in all your glory and with all your faults. It's where you feel accepted exactly as you are and where you accept others for being exactly who they are.

It's not always one-stop shopping. I tried to find my tribe close to home, among the moms in suburban Connecticut. I did meet plenty of nice people. I joined book clubs and attended cocktail parties and sat through endless dinner parties, and you know what? I had fun. I loved many of the people I met.

But I didn't feel that overwhelming sense of acceptance, comfort, and belonging, because I never felt like I could really be myself. There was an unspoken code of conduct that I couldn't seem to adhere to. Sometimes I felt like I was too direct, or too opinionated, or too *something*. Other times I felt not pretty enough, not thin enough, not *something* enough. I didn't wear the right clothes or eat the right foods. The moms in my community all seemed so perfect, with their flawless skin and polished outfits and beautiful high-heeled shoes that never seemed to cause blisters. Meanwhile I was the one standing in the corner at the cocktail party who couldn't walk because my heels were bleeding.

It took trial, error, and patience, but I eventually found my people. And when I did, there was an amazing sense of love and belonging. There's no substitute for finding that group of people with whom you can be totally you and know you'll be accepted exactly as you are.

Who are your people? Where in your life can you take a deep breath, exhale fully, relax your shoulders, and sink into knowing you absolutely belong in that room? If you haven't found that place, know that it's out there for you and it's worth finding.

Here are some things to keep in mind:

✧ Be open to the idea that your tribe may appear in an unexpected place. The women who choose pole dancing as their hobby became one of my most cherished tribes, a sisterhood of kindred spirits. This is not what I envisioned or expected for myself, but as Seinfeld said, "This is me. This is who I am. That's my group."

✧ Practice acceptance and receiving. Be open to the idea that the people you encounter are in your life for a reason, and be receptive to the love and connection available from them. That way, when your tribe appears, you'll be open to them.

✧ Take pleasure in supporting others. Be a genuine cheerleader and enthusiastic supporter to your friends. Be the friend you want to have.

Practice Gratitude

There's a reason everyone's talking about gratitude, from Oprah to Gwyneth and everyone in between. Studies show that practicing gratitude leads to a measurable increase in both happiness and physical health. It's one of the easiest and most surefire ways to prioritize your happiness. Gratitude usually comes in tiny moments...all you need to do is notice them.

You can write the things you are grateful for in a gratitude journal. Also, you can practice sharing three gratitudes per day with a friend to keep them top of mind. You can envision a few things you're grateful for after your morning meditation. The key is to acknowledge them, rather than letting those moments of gratitude slip by.

Noticing things you're grateful for helps keeps you in a state of wonder and awe for the miracle of life and the world in which we live. It's so easy to walk through life without even noticing the beauty of a sunset, or the kindness of a stranger, or the lovely friendship between two toddlers in a playground. When you wake up to little miracles through your gratitude practice, you'll start to notice them everywhere. Your life will be that much richer for it.

Another benefit of gratitude is that it takes your mind out of a state of *wanting more* and moves it to a state of *appreciation for what is.* Rather than focusing on getting up the next rung of the ladder, it shifts your focus back onto the present moment, your life as you're living it right now.

The other day I got so much pleasure from watching a baby bird outside yapping at her mama, waiting to be fed a worm. As soon as the mama bird put the worm in the baby bird's mouth, baby bird swallowed it and then she started yapping again! She wanted another worm! That poor mama put another worm in baby bird's mouth, and the scene repeated again. More yapping; finally, the mama gave her baby one last worm, and then she flew away. Clearly she was completely exhausted by the demands of mothering. It reminded me of my own babies, who had just left for college. I was missing my kids so much in that moment, but witnessing that little interaction brought a smile to my face. I was conscious and mindful enough to notice this precious moment. That's gratitude. And gratitude makes happiness happen.

Find Your Own Thing

Some people say that a state of happiness is achieved when your life is in alignment with who you are and what you want.

The happiest moms I know have something special in their lives that they pursue just for their own personal fulfillment. My friend Lisa has art and painting. My friend Lesley has charity work. My friend Elizabeth has photography. Megan, a gifted singer, joined a band that plays at local restaurants on weekends.

What matters is that *that thing* is fun—that it reflects who you are and what you really want—and that it makes you feel like the best version of yourself. It makes you feel fulfilled, like the best version of you. Doing this activity feels right in your body.

If you don't know what your thing might be, look for clues. They're very easily found in your childhood. What did you love doing as a child? Were you an athlete, a dancer, a bookworm, a little chef? Think back to the activities you could lose yourself in for hours and start there.

Today's To-Dos: In the Pursuit of Happiness

Stay connected with the people in your tribe(s). Try to reach out to at least one person, whether a friend or a family member, each day, even if it's only via text message.

Start writing daily gratitudes in your journal. When you wake up, write down three things you're grateful for. At the end of the day, repeat this exercise. This will help get you into the habit of noticing little moments you're grateful for throughout the day.

What activities make you feel alive? What activities do you need to do more of? Write them down in your journal. What activities that other people do intrigue you? Consider those.

What is your thing? If you don't know yet, brainstorm ideas until you find something you'd like to try or liked in the past. Try it. If it's not right, try something else.

Chapter 14

LISTEN TO YOUR INTUITION

Intuition is the highest form of intelligence,
transcending all individual abilities and skills.

—Sylvia Clare

When Andrew was a toddler, he had pet names for Larry and me. He referred to Larry as the *hard guy* and to me as the *soft lady.* That's because Larry, with his masculine energy, was strong, solid, always busy and charging ahead, whereas I, with my dominant feminine energy, was calm, nurturing, and more intuitive. Larry liked to get things done and then quickly move on to the next thing, whereas I liked to sit with Andrew, read a story, work on a puzzle together, snuggle on the couch. Masculine vs. feminine—doing vs. being. It was a striking enough difference for a toddler to pick up on.

We all have both masculine and feminine qualities within us—both are important. As women, our feminine qualities tend to naturally dominate. However, many of us were raised to abandon our feminine energy and embrace our more masculine sides. Masculine energy qualities are the ones that are valued in our society, especially in the workplace. When women entered the workforce in large numbers in the 1970s and '80s, embracing masculine energy was seen as a way to get ahead in the world. It's like we women thought we could achieve professional parity with men, only by emulating them.

An easy way to understand masculine vs. feminine energy is, as Andrew showed us, simply as hard vs. soft. We need both, but one tends to dominate in each person. Masculine energy is aggressive, assertive, impatient, and analytical. Where's the pleasure in that? Feminine energy is receptive, nurturing, and intuitive.

Our masculine energy is important—it can help us succeed in the workplace and wherever we're striving to get ahead and make things happen in life. But the way to bring pleasure into life is to embrace feminine energy. The feminine is about being rather than doing—attracting rather than achieving. Where is the pleasure in rushing, striving, getting stuff done? But sit back, be present, and be receptive to the beauty that life has to offer in each moment, and you'll discover that pleasure can be found everywhere.

The masculine is all about analyzing and thinking—it's about being in your head. The feminine taps into the wisdom inherent in your body, your intuition.

For me, my body talks to me through feelings, not words. When a decision is right for me, my body feels expansive, light, like I could fly. Sometimes it's accompanied by a feeling of inner knowing, a feeling of rightness, a yes that comes from deep within. When a decision is not right for me, my body feels contracted, heavy, and tense.

I remember the day I "knew" about my business, back when it was just an art project on my dining room table. Feeling creative that day, I played around with the weekly layout, trying to get it just right. At the time, there were already five vertical boxes, one each for mom and up to four kids, but each had equal space. That particular day, I felt as though it could be better, so I took out my ruler and started fiddling around with it. I tried various adjustments, one of which was to make the space for mom about double the height as it was before, making the kids boxes a bit smaller. I looked at my drawing and intuitively, I knew. This would work for moms like me. I knew this was how my planner would be differentiated from every other planner on the market. This is what people mean when they say that sometimes, in certain situations, "you just know."

Interestingly, this big breakthrough didn't come as a result of overthinking or striving to accomplish something. It came from doodling, feeling creative, playing—something from which I derive great pleasure. Since it was pleasurable and my mood was clear, I was receptive, allowing the right answer to come to me at the right time. That's the power of feminine energy and the power of intuition.

If you're confused about your intuition, you're not alone. For years, I thought my intuition was "broken," but the truth was, it was there all along. I just didn't know how to identify it. If you're someone who struggles at all with anxiety it can be especially difficult to identify your intuition because you have so many competing voices in your head, vying for attention.

Here are a few tips that will help you notice the signals from your intuition more clearly:

✧ When you're making a decision, start by relaxing completely. Ask yourself the question and then check in with your body. A yes from your intuition will make you feel expansive and light—a no feels contracting and heavy. I notice this sensation most prominently in my chest and shoulders. A yes feels like my chest expanding out toward the sky, whereas a no feels like my shoulders closing in on me.

✧ Think back to times in your life when your intuition spoke to you very loudly and clearly, like in my example with the *momAgenda* layout, above. What were the sensations you noticed? Was it a quiet voice in your head? A deep knowing within your body? Once you can identify how your intuition communicates, you'll be able to notice it when it speaks more quietly.

✧ Meditate. Meditation helps clear out the background noise in your head, helping you attune to your intuition.

✧ It feels good. Following your intuition is pleasurable, because it feels like you're doing what's in your highest good. Even if it's a choice that makes you sad, such as breaking up with someone you love or ending a long friendship that's grown toxic, following your intuition always feels *right* in your body.

Connect to the Body

In order to listen to your body, it's helpful to start by connecting with it. Start with a body scan. Relax in a comfortable position and close your eyes. Then, place all your attention on your feet. Notice how your feet are feeling. Then move your attention to your calves, thighs, hips, belly, chest, arms, neck, head. Pause at each part of your body and notice how it's feeling—is it relaxed and soft, or clenched and hard? Does it have anything to tell you today? Doing a body scan on a daily basis can help you start to reconnect and listen to your body's wisdom. After doing your body scan, think about a decision you're struggling with, then ask yourself the question, "How does this feel?" Tune in to the sensations in your body for guidance.

You can also connect to your body by dancing, yoga, meditation, and stretching. Feel into the sensations of your body as you move it, rather than just trying to get through it. Try to be present in each moment.

Be Creative

Feminine energy is associated with creative power.

Think beyond traditional forms of creativity and explore ways you may be able to harness your creative energy. It's a misconception that making traditional "art," such as painting or drawing, is the only way to be creative. When I want to be creative, I enjoy dancing, cooking, and writing. Creativity is the act of taking an original idea in your head and making it a reality.

If you don't know how to harness your creativity, think back to activities you enjoyed when you were a young child. I was terrible at drawing and painting in art class, and as a result I thought I wasn't creative. But I loved dance class—no one had a bigger smile on their face than I did during the square dance performance in third grade. Bingo! Dance was the creative outlet that brought me joy as a young child…and it still is.

Create a Sanctuary

Set up a space for yourself in your home where you can feel calm, centered, and special. Fill it with objects that make you feel happy and calm…maybe a picture of your kids, a beautiful scented candle, and a bunch of soft pillows. Keep the lighting soft and muted, include a speaker so you can listen to your favorite music, and add a beautiful, soft throw blanket or something else that makes you feel cozy and protected. It can be a room or a nook or a corner in a room.

You can use this space for self-care: use it to meditate, practice breathing exercises, write in your journal, or plan your week in your day planner. It only takes a few minutes per day to sit quietly and get centered in stillness.

Today's To-Dos: Intuition

Hone your intuition. Journal about intuitive hits that have been correct in your life and what they felt like in your body. Maybe you "just knew" about your spouse, or having a baby, or about your career choice, or about which college you'd go to.

Practice tuning in to your intuition when you have decisions to make, and ask yourself what feels *right* in your body. It's just as important as determining what makes sense from the point of view of your thinking mind.

Chapter 15

THE SECRET SAUCE: PLEASURE

It takes courage to say yes to rest and play in a
culture where exhaustion is seen as a status symbol.

—BRENÉ BROWN

Once you have cleared out space in your life by drawing boundaries, setting priorities, and saying no to everything that's not aligned with your truth, you will be set to receive one of the greatest gifts life has to offer.

That gift is pleasure.

We're hard-wired to seek pleasure and avoid pain. As a species, we seek pleasure—it's in our DNA to want and need pleasure in our lives. Back in the caveman days, if you didn't enjoy and partake in the pleasures afforded by food, water, and sex, you didn't survive and reproduce.

The research that exists on pleasure tells us that there's a direct link between pleasure and good health. Pleasure and its associated positive states of mind actually boost our immune system, while negative states of mind such as stress, worry, and self-sacrifice can be detrimental to our health. Scientists have proven that pleasurable experiences like listening to music or being hugged or having sex can actually directly benefit our health, by boosting immunity and thereby improving our healing powers.

Sadly, pleasure is not prioritized in our culture, especially for women and even more so for moms. Our mothers don't raise us to pursue pleasure. Society doesn't encourage us to pursue pleasure. Pleasure is viewed with suspicion and often derision. It's relegated to the bedroom, after dark, in private. Certain forms of pleasure are so taboo that we're not even supposed to talk about them in polite company.

As women, we're often raised to feel guilty about pleasure. The patriarchal culture for the last five thousand or so years has tried to control and curb women's pleasure. We're taught that pursuing pleasure is hedonistic, or selfish, or morally wrong, that our outsized appetites are "too much" and possibly dangerous. We're taught that a little bit of pleasure is okay, as long as we keep it under control and within the limits of what's considered acceptable by our society. For example, sex is okay, as long as it's not the wrong kind of sex...too much sex, or too casual, or with too many partners, for example. There are actually derogatory words in our culture specifically for women who like sex "too much" or have "too many" partners, such as *slut*; not so for men. Restraint from bodily pleasures is considered a virtue, a sign of moral superiority and self-mastery.

A quick Google search illustrates the puritanical way our culture views pleasure. One article I found stated that happiness is a long-term benefit, coming from hard-won pursuits like graduating from college or completing a marathon, whereas pleasure is a short-term boost that comes from quick fixes like ice cream and alcohol. This statement is implicitly judgmental of pleasure, linking it to potentially addictive substances rather than nobler pursuits.

In addition to being judgmental, it's just plain wrong. Pleasure is the secret sauce to living a happy life. When you prioritize pleasure and fun in your life, you increase your sense of well-being. You feel better, look better, and have more energy. Giving yourself short bursts of pleasure increases your exuberance, improves your mood, and elevates your motivation. You feel more empowered to take positive steps in your life. You have an increased sense of delight and passion for life. You look at life more optimistically and see disappointments as momentary setbacks rather than permanent letdowns. You're able to move on more quickly from losses and failures.

By extension, pleasure empowers us to live more fully. Pleasurable experiences infuse us with the energy and optimism and exuberance to embrace each experience along our journeys.

There are the obvious ways to pursue pleasure, such as dancing, laughing with close friends, and having great sex, but we don't always have the opportunity—or the desire—to indulge in those pleasures every day. So we can pursue smaller, manageable bursts of pleasure throughout the day.

But here's the thing: Pleasure is not derived from taking more vacations or having more money; rather, pleasure is derived from ordinary, everyday, simple experiences in life. Pleasure comes from doing the little things that make you feel good in your body, enjoying connections with other people, noticing the beauty around us, being able to relax and enjoy our families. Pleasure is feeling grateful for what we have rather than longing for what we don't have. It's feeling like you have some measure of control and feeling optimistic about your future. Pleasure is the embodied feeling of day-to-day happiness.

Why We Resist Pleasure

Despite how positive pleasure is, many of us have a complicated relationship with it. Much of that goes back to childhood conditioning that taught us that we must have permission to pursue pleasure. As children, we depended on our parents for pleasure. For example, we had to ask permission to do pleasurable things, like eat (especially extra-pleasurable foods like desserts), play with friends, or buy a new game or toy. We were also dependent on our caretakers for more intangible sources of pleasure, such as love, nurturing, acceptance, and a sense of belonging. As adults, we may subconsciously feel guilty for pursuing pleasure because we no longer have someone's permission. And we're never taught that pleasure is our birthright and that we alone are responsible for ensuring we're experiencing pleasure in our lives and that we no longer need permission to pursue it.

In addition, we may avoid pleasure because of an old childhood belief that it won't please our caregivers. Our parents raised us to work hard and become productive members of society, feeding us the myth that hard work and perseverance are the exclusive paths to happiness. As kids that meant going to school and working our hardest, sometimes sacrificing fun for the sake of succeeding. Because we crave the approval of our parents, we bend ourselves backward to look good to them, pushing pleasure aside in favor of doing things that will earn our parents' approval.

I remember my stepfather scoffing at me for planning an outfit for an upcoming dance when I was thirteen. I felt excited about the upcoming dance and thought it was fun to plan an outfit that would make me feel pretty. He thought it was "silly" and a "waste of time" for someone of my intelligence to expend energy on my fashion choices. Apparently, I was expected to spend every moment of my life using my brainpower for more noble pursuits than pleasure. We internalize this conditioning, that pleasure is a selfish, indulgent, petty pursuit, and it makes it more difficult for us, as adults, to enjoy the pleasures in life. Even something as innocuous as taking Advil for a headache was frowned upon. Why couldn't I just tough it out? My response tended to be, why would I do that? Why deny yourself pain relief when it's available and relatively inexpensive? I had similar conversations when it was time to consider pain relief during childbirth. The prevailing attitude among the doctors and nurses was that it would be prudent to wait as long as possible in the birth to receive an epidural. There was an absolute sense of superiority to waiting as long as possible or even foregoing pain relief. This confused me. Why wouldn't you avail yourself of pain relief when it's available and it doesn't harm you or your baby?

The *no pain, no gain* mentality stuck with many of us. That's the widely held belief that the good things in life take hard work, sacrifice, or some other cost. The good things in life can't possibly be easy or come naturally…we must fight, struggle, and emerge triumphant from battle in order to reap the rewards that are the pleasures in life.

As moms, we're especially resistant to pleasure. The idea that pleasure is "selfish" plays directly into moms' tendency to put others first. We're afraid that pleasure for ourselves will mean we have less to give to our kids, that paying attention to ourselves means we'll have less attention to give to our kids. In our zero-sum-game mentality, more pleasure for us means less (time, energy, attention, you name it) for our kids.

This bias doesn't just come from our own homes—it's pervasive in our society. We live in a culture in which moms who sacrifice themselves and their own pleasure are considered good moms, whereas those who prioritize their own pleasure, their own voices, and their own needs are considered narcissists.

The truth is, there's an unlimited supply of happiness, pleasure, love, and energy in the universe. It's not a zero-sum game, where more for you means less for your kids. On the contrary, the happier and more pleasured you are, the *more* you'll have to give to your kids. Think about it: When you feel down and low-energy, you don't have as much to give. But when you're feeling fulfilled and happy, you have a surplus of energy to give. You have more to give your kids, your work, your friends, everything in your life. Fill your own tank first and watch as your abundance increases in every area of your life.

Do Things You Enjoy

If you want to enjoy your life, make it a priority to do the things that bring you pleasure and happiness on a more regular basis. When we deny our own needs, including our need for pleasure, life can start to feel really *blah*. Vague depression can follow. Before we know it, the couch is calling our names pretty much all the time.

Engage in activities that make you feel alive and connected, like art, movies, music, travel, or cooking. Take a moment and stop and think: *What makes you feel alive and engaged with the world or what activities do you think might do so?*

Then prioritize it. Prioritizing pleasure means saying *this matters*. It means making the time and committing yourself to spending more time doing things you love doing. Maybe you only have half an hour per week to do the things you enjoy. Don't waste that half-hour scrolling through your social media accounts! Free time is a premium; it's important to be intentional about how you spend it.

Some of us think it's silly to engage in activities purely for pleasure. *It's silly*, or *that's a waste of time*. I beg to differ! Pleasure is part of what makes the journey worthwhile. Life is hard, and we all struggle at times in our lives. Pleasure reminds us that life is good and beautiful. Even during our struggles, we can enjoy little pleasures like a beautiful song or a delicious meal. We can get pleasure out of pets or even just observing what's happening in nature outside our homes.

Are you spending time engaged in activities that bring you pleasure and happiness? If not, change that.

Be Discerning: Choose Healthy Pleasure Practices

A big part of self-care is knowing which pleasure practices are healthy for you. The way to know if a particular form of pleasure is healthy is to ask yourself two questions:

1. Does this harm another person?

2. Does this harm me or have side effects that may harm me?

Pleasure that harms you or has side effects that can harm you can be tricky to discern. Oftentimes, we choose pleasure practices that are highly pleasurable in moderation but self-destructive when we overindulge.

Eating a small piece of dark chocolate is pleasurable. Eating an entire chocolate cake is likely to give you a stomach-ache. Drinking one glass of wine can be pleasurable, but polishing off the whole bottle in one sitting may have side effects that are not. Enjoying a delicious meal while reconnecting with your partner at the end of the day is pleasurable—on the other hand, it's hard to feel real sensual pleasure while mindlessly scarfing down a quick meal in front of the TV.

A note about addictions. When we compulsively indulge in certain substances or experiences such as alcohol and drugs in order to mask our anxieties, that's not a pleasure practice. Pleasure makes you feel more alive. It keeps you connected to all the wonderful people and experiences that life has to offer. It wakes up all the senses in your body, and helps you take note of the beauty in the world around us. Addictions, on the other hand, serve to numb the addict from the world around her. When you're addicted, you're checked out and disconnected from life. Addictions and unhealthy pleasures are an escape from reality, whereas healthy pleasure helps you embrace reality, and live and enjoy every moment of your life.

Healthy pleasure is all about embracing the beauty and joy of your life, celebrating your one unique life and making it the best it can possibly be. It's about having experiences that enrich you, maintaining deep connections with loved ones, and giving your senses the tastes, sounds, smells, and feelings they desire most. It's about tuning in and waking up in your body. It's about feeling alive, and radiating that aliveness out into the world.

Prioritize Pleasure

One of the highest forms of self-care is to indulge in pleasure every day. Make every day pleasurable. One way to do this is to decide to treat yourself as though it's your birthday. What do you do for yourself on your birthday? Maybe you make yourself a special breakfast, serve yourself fresh blueberries from the farmers' market, make coffee in your favorite mug. You probably would wear something that makes you feel special and beautiful, and you'd carry yourself with a little more confidence and joy. Maybe you'd treat yourself to a latte in the morning…and a nap in the afternoon. Maybe you'd put music and a candle on while making dinner, because that makes it more fun. The point is to treat yourself with this much love and care *every day*.

This is the heart of pleasure. Eating delicious food; enjoying amazing, connected sex; listening to the most beautiful music; wearing clothing that makes you feel beautiful. These little pleasures fill your tank and create happiness.

(And speaking of things that feel good…)

Sleep is my sexual fantasy.—Lori B.

When it comes to sex—a type of pleasure that encompasses the biological, the physical, the emotional, and sometimes even the spiritual—how many moms don't even want to have it anymore? I've lost count of the number of married or partnered women I've spoken to who've decided they'd be fine without ever having sex again, or who only have sex out of a sense of obligation to their partner. We cut ourselves off from one of the most profound and all-encompassing pleasures of life. But why?

I don't know the answer, but I do know it's a real phenomenon. When you're a mom, especially a mom with young kids, sex seems to take a backseat to nearly everything else. We have the demands of kids, work, running the household, and whatever else we're dealing with. Those of us at home with the kids have them climbing all over us and taking up all our physical and emotional energy. At night we get into bed and ask ourselves, "Sex or sleep?" Sleep nearly always wins. Same thing in the morning. Sleep late on a Sunday, or have sex? It's not even a contest when the kids are young, and you're exhausted and overwhelmed.

There are so many reasons to have sex, and yet we come up with so many excuses not to.

Sex feels good. Sex helps us bond with our partners in a way we don't bond with anyone else, forging a shared intimacy and closeness you can't get through any other means, ultimately strengthening the relationship. Sex is good for your physical health: it gets the endorphins flowing, boosts your immune system, and helps relieve stress. It's also good for your emotional health—people in good sexual relationships have less depression, less anxiety, and higher self-esteem than those who aren't. Oh, and besides all those scientific benefits, it's fun.

And yet. Some of us enjoy healthy sex lives, but a significant portion of moms report that sex is one more thing on a long to-do list of tasks that feel more like obligations. At the end of a long day, the last thing we want is yet another person touching us or wanting something from us. We give and give all day, whether we're at work or at home with the kids. We do everything, it seems: we take care of the kids, we go to work, and we take care of all the emotional labor. Sex feels like one more thing we have to do, one more thing we're giving to another person. It ceases being a shared, exquisitely pleasurable experience and becomes a duty, an obligation performed once a week or once a month or, if this goes on for too long, once or twice a year. And there's nothing sexy or even remotely appealing about that.

I'm happy to report from personal experience that as the kids get older, your sex drive can, and most likely will, return. If you had a good sex drive before kids, you'll have one again. The period during which the kids demand all your physical and emotional energy is short, in the scheme of things.

Put It on the Calendar

Before kids, sex tends to happen naturally. You're hanging out, minding your own business doing stuff around the house, and boom, all of a sudden you're in bed enjoying a Saturday afternoon. After kids, these spontaneous moments become more and more rare. The answer is to put it in your calendar.

Scheduling sex may sound like the least romantic idea you've ever heard, but hear me out. You schedule in all your priorities, right? I schedule in all my important commitments, such as meetings, school pickups, workouts, and get-togethers with friends. I know in my own life, if I don't schedule my workouts, they don't happen. So why wouldn't you schedule in one of the most important things to maintain your relationship with your partner?

It takes effort to reconnect with your sexuality after you've had kids, especially if your sexuality is a part of you that you've temporarily given up on. Just like engaging in the act itself, getting in the mood doesn't happen naturally as often as it used to—it takes a conscious decision on your part to make it happen.

Scheduling it may even help you get in the mood. Let's say you schedule sex for Saturday night. You may find yourself thinking about it during the day on Saturday, maybe even looking forward to it. Maybe you'll put on a pretty bra or a sexy outfit for date night that night, just to make yourself feel sexy. Maybe you'll send your partner a text letting him know you're thinking about your night together. The planning and anticipation can become part of the fun.

Anticipation can create more opportunities for getting in the mood. Treat yourself to beautiful underwear that makes you feel sexy. Take a bubble bath and savor the feeling of warm water on your skin. Read an erotic novel. Talk about sex with your friends or your partner. Listen to a sex-focused podcast or to music that puts you in the mood. Wear an outfit that makes you feel amazing. Light a candle and turn down the lights to set a sexy mood in your bedroom.

Your physical connection is the superglue that holds a happy relationship together. Don't leave it to chance.

Banish the G Word: Guilt

Don't let guilt stop you from enjoying pleasure. Ignore that term: *guilty pleasure*. By calling it a guilty pleasure, we're assigning guilt to those who enjoy that pleasure and telling each other (and ourselves) that this pleasure is bad in some way. This sets up an unhealthy relationship with that pleasure.

Healthy pleasure is not necessarily what our modern society says it "should" be. There are social norms that tell us how we're supposed to behave, what we're supposed to like and not like, and even with whom we're supposed to have sex. In matriarchal societies, where women are at the center of the social structure, people are not made to feel guilty about their sexual desires. No one should be made to feel guilty about their preferences, as long as they're not hurting anyone.

We live in a patriarchal society, where women are expected to sacrifice themselves and their needs when they become moms. We're told we're not deserving of self-care, of taking the time to take care of ourselves, of attending to our own needs. That's why self-care is such a revolutionary act. It's saying, *I matter. I'm going to take care of myself, and I'm not going to feel guilty about it. I deserve to treat myself and do the things that make me feel good.*

Today's To-Dos: What's Your Pleasure?

Prioritize pleasure. Make it a goal to pursue pleasure every day. It doesn't have to take a lot of time—it could be as simple as treating yourself to a new lip gloss. Keep yourself accountable by writing your daily pleasure in your journal each day.

Set up a spot in your home that's just for you. It could be as simple as a corner or a closet in your bedroom, or it could be an entire room in your home. Make it cozy, warm, and inviting.

Make an appointment to do something special for yourself at least once a week. Write it in your planner in pen. Whether it's a manicure, a massage, or a good book, make it something that makes you feel pampered.

PUTTING IT
ALL TOGETHER

*The biggest adventure you can take is
to live the life of your dreams.*

—OPRAH WINFREY

In psychology, there are four separate stages of learning known as the *four stages of competence*. These are stages we move through on our journey to deeper understanding or mastery of something new.

During the first stage, *unconscious incompetence*, we're unaware of what we don't know. This is the stage of blissful ignorance, where the saying "you don't know what you don't know" is applicable. Let's say you've developed the habit of eating a whole bag of gummy bears every day. At the unconscious incompetence phase, it's simply never occurred to you that gummy bears have tons of sugar and may be contributing to your weight struggles or health issues or tooth decay. And if someone suggested to you that your gummy bear habit may not be beneficial to you in the long term, you might disagree.

At the second stage, *conscious incompetence*, you start to recognize what you previously were unaware of, though you don't know what to do about it. In the example we're using, you become aware that gummy bears are filled with sugar and may be exacerbating certain health issues you've been struggling with. You know you're doing something that needs changing, but you don't yet know how to change it.

At the third stage, *conscious competence*, you know what the problem is and you know what needs to be done about it, but you need concentration and conscious awareness in order to take those actions. In the example above, you might put together an eating plan that eliminates gummy bears or you might go to the store and look for alternatives that are lower in sugar or you might start tracking your food intake. The point is, you know what to do and you're practicing it each day. You have to put in effort at this stage and remind yourself to take the actions you've committed to.

The fourth stage is the stage of *unconscious competence*. At this stage, you've gotten so much practice in your new skill that you no longer need to think about it, because it's now second nature. In our example, you no longer buy gummy bears when you go to the store, or really even think about gummy bears—they're simply no longer a part of your life. It feels better to eat other things now.

Many, many moms today are walking around in stage one, unconscious incompetence. These moms are not feeling happy, fulfilled, or peaceful, but they think this is a normal state of being at this stage of life. They don't have any awareness that what they're experiencing can change, that a better life is possible. They may be resigned to waiting it out until things get better as the kids grow older and there are fewer demands on them.

A large group of moms is also in the conscious incompetence category. These moms know they're overwhelmed and sad, just as I was when I first met Sherry, but they might not know exactly why they feel that way. They may see other moms who are already putting themselves back on the to-do list and wonder what their secret is. They may be asking themselves, *Why is it that I have everything I ever wanted, and yet I feel empty inside?* They also may be guilting themselves about their own feelings. *Who am I to be unhappy when I have a spouse and healthy kids and a roof over my head?*

It takes effort, both in terms of energy and practice, to make the transition from stage two to stage three, conscious competence. This is the stage where, with concentration and effort, you can start putting certain practices into action in your life. Reading this book, and taking the steps outlined here, is an amazing way to start practicing conscious competence. So are reading other books, listening to podcasts, journaling, meditating, and practicing the steps discussed here like saying no, drawing boundaries, setting priorities, and finding pleasure in everyday activities. It's natural, during this stage, to sometimes feel frustrated or like the task is too difficult. You're making major shifts in your ways of thinking and your life, and doing so rarely feels comfortable. The most important thing at this phase is to stay focused and not give up. It does get easier!

The more you practice, the stronger your inner muscles will become. The pinnacle we're all striving for is unconscious competence, the stage where it's second nature for you to think of yourself as well as your kids when you make your to-do-list, plan your day, and consider taking on new commitments. At this stage, you've made putting yourself back into the equation a part of your life. You view yourself as a whole person, with needs and desires separate from those of your kids and partner. You have your own interests and creative pursuits. You've identified the habits and routines that help you be at your best, and you've incorporated them into your life. You say no to things that aren't aligned with your priorities; you have clear boundaries about how you want others to treat you. At this stage, remember we're aiming for progress rather than perfection.

Bottom Line: It's All about You

Way back when Sherry and I started together, she said to me, "It's time to put yourself back in the equation."

Back in 2010, I didn't know what that meant. And while I've done a ton of work on myself, even now, I continue to be a work in progress. But I finally figured out how to put myself back in the equation—looking back, I finally realize exactly what Sherry meant.

I spent years focusing on everyone else, trying to make everyone happy, tending to their needs, not my own. I spent years focusing outside myself, entirely on other people. I spent years erasing myself from the equation.

At this moment in time, I totally get it. And *I'm* back on *my* to-do list. Finally.

Does this story ring true for you? From the minute your babies were babies, you've been highly attuned to their every need and desire. You've been able to read their signals, whether it's the looks on their faces or the intonations of their cries, and know whether they needed food or water or a sweater or a diaper change. You and your babies communicated almost telepathically during those early years, and you learned to rely on those unspoken signals for important information that would help you take the best possible care of your children.

As your babies grew older, your focus was still on them. You were watching to see if they were happy at school, whether they got along with their friends, or felt comfortable in their classroom. It seems never-ending, the amount of watching and observing you do as a mom, in order to ensure your children are happy and healthy and thriving in the world.

As a result of this evolutionary process, which feels as natural and effortless as breathing, we can easily lose ourselves. When we start to place our focus outside ourselves and onto our kids, we can lose our sense of self and begin to erase ourselves and our needs from being considered.

I'll be fine no matter what, we think. *What matters is that the kids are happy.*

Over time, that thinking can expand beyond your kids to your spouse, your friends, your mother, your babysitter, and the PTA. All of a sudden, you're taking care of everyone else and highly attuned to the needs of everyone else, and ignoring your own needs.

Let's rewrite that story. It's time to put the focus back on you.

It's time to say, "I matter. My voice matters. My opinions, my desires, my needs, my happiness matter."

Putting this into practice is simple, although it's not always easy.

Start thinking about what you want and what you need. You may not even be able to identify what you want or need at this point. That's okay...it will come over time. The more you consider your own needs, the more you'll become attuned to them—just like you're attuned to your children's needs.

I'm not saying think about you instead of them. I'm saying think about you *in addition to* them. *You can take care of your kids and still take care of yourself.*

What Do You Really Want?

> *If you don't know where you're going, any road will get you there.*
>
> —LEWIS CARROLL

What do you really want? What are your desires? So often, our desires are actually other people's desires or they revolve around other people's needs. We all desire for our kids to get what they want and be happy. But what do you desire for *you?* You're allowed to have desires of your own, even during the years you're raising your kids. One way we erase ourselves from the equation is by letting go of our desires for ourselves and putting all our thoughts and hopes onto our kids and partners.

Try this:

Get your journal and make a list of your desires: all the things you really want, with regard to your body, mind, spirit, career, relationships, and family. Let your desires be outlandish. Once you've made your list, make it visual. Create a Pinterest board or a vision board at home, with pictures of the things you desire, and visit your visual representation frequently to remind yourself of what you really want.

I'm not talking about goals, which are different from desires. Goals are things you work toward and take definitive steps toward achieving. Desires are things you simply *want*. You don't have to know how to get them, and very often the steps toward achieving them won't be evident at first. Desires are longings in your body. Just that feeling of longing and wanting is what I want you to bring back to your consciousness. Remember what it feels like to really want something for yourself. By the simple act of wanting it, of feeling that longing deep in your being, you create fertile ground for it to come to you.

Your desires represent the life you really and truly want. They're your authentic self, speaking to you. So it's very important, when thinking about your desires, to do the work outlined in this book first. If you're still having a hard time drawing boundaries or setting priorities, you may still be living with your focus on others rather than on you. In such cases it may be difficult to discern your authentic truth with clarity through the clouds of other people's opinions. In addition, many of us live in denial of what we truly want because we don't think we're allowed to want it. By doing the work outlined in this book, you'll slowly move out of denial and be more ready to face the reality of what's true in your life and the changes you really want to make to put yourself back in the equation.

You'll know you're really ready to start your desire list when you know with absolute certainty that it's safe to have these desires. That you are allowed to want things for yourself. That it isn't selfish, or wrong, or narcissistic to be a mom who wants to be a whole and happy and fulfilled human being.

Think of your desires as your North Star. Your desires may seem as far away as that distant, bright light, but being in touch with them and keeping your eye on them increases the likelihood that you'll adjust your movements, sometimes consciously and sometimes subconsciously, until you're heading in the right direction.

It's Not Magic

Some people think desires are magic, that by writing down and feeling our desires we can manifest them into reality. Although I'm open to that being true, I'm more of a pragmatist at heart. When you've written down your desires and solidified in your mind and body what you really want, and made a safe space for yourself to want those things, you start noticing opportunities to get them. You make shifts in your behavior, sometimes not even consciously, to get closer to your desires.

You'll also start taking bolder steps toward realizing your desires. If one of your desires is to have a deeper, more connected, and more fulfilling sex life, but you haven't been able to articulate that, doing the work in this book might allow you to shift the focus away from the outside world and onto yourself, to focus on your needs and what you really want, and help you see that it's perfectly valid to want it. By facing that truth, you'll be more likely to take steps toward making it happen. Perhaps it will inspire you to make an appointment with a couple's therapist, and start having real conversations with your partner. Maybe you'll go to individual therapy and do the work on yourself necessary to be truly vulnerable with your partner, a necessary condition to real intimacy. Maybe you'll pick up a book and start reading about tantric sex practices. Whatever steps you take, by acknowledging the desire, you create the conditions that make it possible to bring it closer to reality, and you empower yourself to take action.

Whatever your desire is, the steps in this book will help you create the space in your life to make it a reality, to give yourself permission to take the time necessary to research and develop your idea, and flush out the steps to fulfilling your desire.

Keep in mind that what you write on your desire list is only a starting point. Be open-minded about how your desires will come to fruition. They certainly may not look exactly the way you think they're going to look, and that's okay.

One of the reasons we live our lives around everyone else's desires is that it feels safe. It's safer to help everyone else realize their dreams than to go out and try to capture our own. Deciding what you really want and going after it is not always going to be a safe, smooth road. There will be bumps along the way and you may question yourself. That's why it's so important to have your own personal North Star, your desire list, always pointing you in the right direction and reassuring you of the rightness of your desires.

How Happy Do You Want to Be?

A friend recounted a conversation she had with her sponsor in a twelve-step program. My friend had stubbornly resisted making certain changes in her life that would have eased the way toward feeling more solid in her sobriety. Then her sponsor asked her this question: *"How happy and healthy to do you want to be?"*

How happy and healthy do you want to be? Do you want to be a little bit happy, a little bit healthy? Do you want to be sort of happy? Do you want to be moderately happy? Or do you want to be as happy and healthy as you can possibly be? Do you want to live your best, most glorious life during your short time here on this planet?

When you encounter resistance to your self-care program, whether from others or from within yourself, ask yourself that question. *How happy and healthy do I want to be?* When you don't feel like going to bed at your regular bedtime because you want to keep watching your favorite show, rather than getting your full eight hours of sleep, ask it. When you're out with friends and tempted to have a few too many drinks, ask it. When it seems easier to say yes than to say no, ask it. *How happy and healthy do I want to be?*

The other night, I was out with my group of friends from college. I see these friends a handful of times per year. At a certain point, I realized that I'd been there a while, and if I didn't leave soon, I'd miss the last train home. It was a decision point: stay out too late, drink too much, not get enough sleep, and feel crappy all the next day (and, let's face it, probably the day after—hangovers last two days for me now). Or call it a night, sleep till 9:00 a.m., and have a beautiful Saturday? I chose the latter. It was the healthiest choice for me, but not the choice I would have made a few years ago. As a result, I enjoyed my time with my friends, *and* I enjoyed the remainder of my weekend.

That brings us back to what this book is all about: the idea that saying no to others is, very often, a way of saying yes to yourself. It comes back to the idea that self-care isn't about a one-time indulgence like a manicure or a bubble bath—it's about making choices every day and every night that ensure you're feeling your best. It's about having the discipline to say no to things that will wreck your weekend, even if those things may seem fun in the moment. It's about fiercely protecting your happiness by deciding what's important to you and focusing your time and attention on that, rather than diluting your energy by spreading it across every task that's asked of you.

But most of all, it's about loving yourself and cherishing yourself so much that you put your own needs at the top of your to-do list. Because you understand at the deepest level that you can't take care of anyone else, not your kids or your partner or anyone else, until you take care of yourself. And that when you do take care of yourself, you have a surplus of love and energy and happiness to share with the people you love.

By doing this work to put yourself back in the equation, by saying you matter, you're giving your kids the gift of a mom who is a whole person, living in her wholeness and her truth. You're setting an example for your kids to, someday in the future, parent their own children in the same manner, with love and attention to themselves as well as their kids.

Make the Commitment

Commitment means being dedicated to something. It means you've gone beyond thinking about it and talking about it and writing about it, and you're actually putting it into practice each day.

Making the commitment to your self-care means you've decided, unequivocally, that you matter, and that you're making choices now and in the future that reflect that. Making the commitment means making hard choices sometimes—saying no even when it's difficult to do so. Breaking out of your comfort zone, and making different choices than the ones you've made before. Making decisions that don't always make everyone else happy all the time.

Your comfort zone is where you've been living for a long time. It feels safe there. But it's also stagnant. Real change and growth don't happen in your comfort zone—they come when you're willing to do things that are uncomfortable and hard.

I'm reminded of the time my youngest son, Jamie, signed up for an academic program abroad the summer after his freshman year in high school. When it came time to board the plane, he panicked and didn't want to go—all of a sudden, he realized life was going to change dramatically and he'd rather stay home with his beloved family and friends and play video games all summer. To convince him to get on the plane, I reminded him of why he signed up for this trip: he wanted to expand his worldview, meet new friends, and have new experiences. Sure enough, he experienced more change and growth over that summer that I can even describe, including (but not limited to) meeting lifelong friends from all over the world and meeting his first girlfriend! That never would have happened had he chosen to stay home that summer. It was an important lesson in doing hard things, getting out of his comfort zone, and embracing change and growth.

Breaking out of your comfort zone to get what you really want takes focus and self-control. It's important to know your *why* so that you don't slip back into old habits. Why do you want to break free of the mom-life crisis? Why do you want to put you back in the equation? What will your life look like after you do so? How are you going to feel? How will you benefit, and how will your family benefit? Take some time to journal on what you want your result to be and why you want that result. Then, as you take the actions outlined in this book, stay focused on the bigger picture of what you really want and why you want it. This will help you stay focused and stay committed when it gets hard and uncomfortable.

There will be moments when you slip back into old habits, and that's okay. It's a part of life to learn as we go, and we're all humans on a journey of understanding. Just get back on track as soon as you realize it. Know that once you start on this journey and get a taste of how good life can feel when you're taking care of you, you'll never want to go back.

You've got this.

RESOURCES

Altucher, James. "Try One or All of These if You Want to Add Value to Your Life." JamesAltucher.com. https://jamesaltucher.com/blog/most-valuable-things-everyone/.

Benhaiem, Annabel. "What This Researcher Discovered after Years of Studying Matriarchal Societies." Huffpost.com, October 10, 2019. https://www.huffpost.com/entry/what-this-researcher-discovered-after-years-of-studying-matriarchal-societies_n_5d-9f60bfe4b06ddfc515f767?ncid=tweetlnkushpmg00000050.

Boguhn, Ally. "Giving Up on Guilty Pleasures: 4 Reasons to Stop Feeling Guilty about Things You Like." *Everyday Feminism,* January 2, 2015. https://everydayfeminism.com/2015/01/guilty-pleasures/.

Breus, Michael J. "The Latest on Blue Light and Sleep." The Sleep Doctor, DABSM, November 6, 2017. https://thesleepdoctor.com/2017/11/06/latest-blue-light-sleep/.

Calhoun, Ada. "The New Midlife Crisis: Why (and How) It's Hitting Gen X Women." Oprah.com. http://www.oprah.com/sp/new-midlife-crisis.html.

Cole, Terri. "Saying Is Believing? Demystifying the Art of Affirmations." TerriCole.com, January 13, 2013.

https://www.terricole.com/
saying-is-believing-demystifying-the-art-of-affirmations/.

"Conscious Competence Learning Model."
Businessballs.com.
https://static1.squarespace.com/static/5569e19fe4b02fd687f77b0f/t/5aad8499352f-533ca549cc94/1521321113919/conscious+competence.pdf.

"Consequences of Insufficient Sleep." Division of Sleep
Medicine at Harvard Medical School, harvard.edu. http://
healthysleep.med.harvard.edu/healthy/matters/consequences.

Delgado, Jennifer. "Science Confirms: Dancing Makes You
Happy." Psychology Spot.
https://psychology-spot.com/dancing-makes-me-happy/.

DNews. "Why Music Makes You Happy." Seeker.com,
January 10, 2011.
https://www.seeker.com/why-music-makes-you-happy-1765157098.html.

Druckerman, Pamela. "What You Learn in Your 40s." *New
York Times,* February 28, 2014.
https://www.nytimes.com/2014/03/01/opinion/
sunday/what-you-learn-in-your-40s.html.

Escalante, Alison. "Mothers Are Drowning in Stress."
Psychology Today, March 6, 2019.
https://www.psychologytoday.com/us/blog/should-storm/201903/mothers-are-drowning-in-stress?utm_source=FacebookPost&utm_medium=FBPost&utm_cam-

paign=FBPost&fbclid=IwAR1Uz4hgc4pAn_DQSQEXc_
Ly480nd9lHduLub2HHzgLykAICrbqiyGpHbCQ.

Falconer, Erin. "How to Eliminate the 'Shoulds' from Your
Life." Mariashriver.com, 2020.
https://mariashriver.com/how-to-eliminate-the-shoulds-
from-your-life/. Reprinted (or adapted) with permission from Erin Falconer, How to Get Sh*t Done (New
York: North Star Way/Simon & Schuster, 2018).

Franzen, Alexandra, "How to Say 'No' to Everything
Ever." AlexandraFranzen.com, February 3, 2013.
http://www.alexandrafranzen.com/2013/02/03/
how-to-say-no-to-everything-ever/.

Grant, Adam, and Alison Sweet Grant. "We Need to Talk
about 'The Giving Tree." *New York Times,* October 1, 2019.
https://parenting.nytimes.com/parent-life/adam-grant-ad-
vice-children?type=roundup&link=intro&te=1&nl=nyt-par-
enting&emc=edit_ptg_20191005?campaign_id=118&in-
stance_id=12857&segment_id=17621&user_id=fa31e-
8134cd978ac0e473ffb68c65610&regi_id=68049158.

Halliwell, Rachel. "Why Dancing Feels So Good." *The
Telegraph,* April 29, 2016.
https://www.telegraph.co.uk/good-news/
seven-seas/why-dancing-feels-good/.

Hill, Jay. "Are You Living for Happiness or Pleasure? They
Are Different!" Lifehack.org.
https://www.lifehack.org/521591/
are-you-living-for-happiness-pleasure-they-are-different.

Kay, Katty, and Claire Shipman. "The Confidence Gap." *The Atlantic,* May, 2014. https://www.theatlantic.com/magazine/archive/2014/05/the-confidence-gap/359815/.

Lang, Susan S. "'Mindless Autopilot' Drives People to Dramatically Underestimate How Many Daily Food Decisions They Make, Cornell Study Finds." *Cornell Chronicle,* December 22, 2006. https://news.cornell.edu/stories/2006/12/mindless-autopilot-drives-people-underestimate-food-decisions.

Lockman, Darcy. "What Good Dads Get Away With." *New York Times,* May 4, 2019. https://www.nytimes.com/2019/05/04/opinion/sunday/men-parenting.html.

Loria, Kevin. "Being Outside Can Improve Memory, Fight Depression, and Lower Blood Pressure—Here Are 12 Science-Backed Reasons to Spend More Time Outdoors." Business Insider, August 22, 2018. https://www.businessinsider.com/why-spending-more-time-outside-is-healthy-2017-7.

Mac, Lyn. "3 Ways to Tap into the Feminine." Huffpost.com, February 12, 2017. https://www.huffpost.com/entry/5-ways-to-tap-into-the-fe_b_9204616.

Manning-Schaffel, Vivian. "5 Reasons to Go Outside, Even When It's Freezing." NBCNews.com, February 3, 2018. https://www.nbcnews.com/better/health/5-good-reasons-go-outside-even-when-it-s-freezing-ncna843331.

Manson, Mark. "Fuck Yes or No." MarkManson.net. https://markmanson.net/fuck-yes.

McKay, Brett, and Kate McKay. "The Eisenhower Decision Matrix: How to Distinguish between Urgent and Important Tasks and Make Real Progress in Your Life." Artofmanliness. com, October 23, 2013. https://www.artofmanliness.com/articles/ eisenhower-decision-matrix/.

Ornish, Dean. "Can Online Communities Be Healing?" Huffpost.com, November 19, 2013. https://www.huffpost.com/entry/ online-communities-health_b_3953766.

Parker-Pope, Tara. "How to Be a Better Friend." *New York Times.* https://www.nytimes.com/guides/smarterliving/how-to-be-a-better-friend?te=1&nl=well&emc=edit_hh_20191107?-campaign_id=18&instance_id=13658&segment_id=18581&user_id=51bdfa4d604942099315d23884c-7b3ce&regi_id=47795440&redirect=true.

Seppälä, Emma. "Connect to Thrive." *Psychology Today,* August 26, 2012. https://www.psychologytoday.com/us/blog/ feeling-it/201208/connect-thrive.

———. "How to Say No Like a Boss." *Psychology Today,* November 1, 2018. https://www.psychologytoday.com/us/blog/ feeling-it/201811/how-say-no-boss.

Sivers, Derek. "No 'Yes.' Either 'Hell Yeah!' or 'No.'" Sivers. org, August 26, 2009. https://sivers.org/hellyeah. Reprinted with permission from Derek Sivers, Anything You Want (New York: Penguin Publishing Group, 2015).

Tartakovsky, Margarita. "A Technique for Feeling Painful Feelings." PsychCentral.com, July 8, 2018. https://psychcentral.com/ blog/a-technique-for-feeling-painful-feelings/.

Thompson, Kelli. "Read This if You Struggle with Trusting Your Gut." ThriveGlobal.com, February 24, 2019. https://thriveglobal.com/stories/ ever-wish-you-would-have-trusted-your-gut-read-this/.

Thorpe, Matthew. "12 Science-Based Benefits of Meditation." Healthline.com, July 5, 2017. https://www.healthline.com/ nutrition/12-benefits-of-meditation.

Walton, Alice G. "A Key to Happiness May Be 'Feeling Your Feelings,' Even the Negative Ones." *Forbes,* August 14, 2017. https://www.forbes.com/sites/alicegwalton/2017/08/14/ a-key-to-happiness-may-be-feeling-your-feel- ings-even-the-negative-ones/#6eafae03637e.

Widrich, Leo. "What Happens to Our Brains When We Exercise and How It Makes Us Happier." Fastcompnay.com, February 4, 2014. https://www.fastcompany.com/3025957/what-happens-to- our-brains-when-we-exercise-and-how-it-makes-us-happier.

Wise, Abigail. "Here's Proof Going Outside Makes You Healthier." Huffpost.com, December 6, 2017. https://www.huffpost.com/entry/how-the-outdoors-make-you_n_5508964.

Zucker, Rebecca. "How to Deal with Constantly Feeling Overwhelmed." *Harvard Business Review,* October 10, 2019. https://hbr.org/2019/10/how-to-deal-with-constantly-feeling-overwhelmed?utm_campaign=hbr&utm_medium=social&utm_source=twitter.

BOOKS

Beattie, Melody. *Codependent No More: How to Stop Controlling Others and Start Caring for Yourself.* Center City, MN: Hazelden Publishing, 1986.

Beck, Martha. *Steering by Starlight: The Science and Magic of Finding Your Destiny.* Emmaus, PA: Rodale Books, 2009.

Fletcher, Emily. *Stress Less, Accomplish More: Meditation for Extraordinary Performance.* New York: HarperCollins, 2020.

Franzen, Alexandra. *How to Say "No": Guidance, Tips, and Email Scripts for 8 Common Scenarios.* Self-published, 2017. http://www.alexandrafranzen.com/wp-content/uploads/2017/01/how-to-say-no_free-workbook_franzen.pdf.

Hartley, Gemma. *Fed Up: Emotional Labor, Women, and the Way Forward.* New York: HarperCollins, 2018.

How Al-Anon Works for Families and Friends of Alcoholics. Virginia Beach, VA: Al-Anon Family Groups, 1995.

Katie, Byron, and Stephen Mitchell. *Loving What Is: Four Questions That Can Change Your Life.* New York: Harmony Books, 2002.

Kay, Katty, and Claire Shipman. *The Confidence Code: The Science and Art of Self-Assurance—What Women Should Know.* New York, HarperCollins, 2014.

Pasricha, Neil. *The Happiness Equation: Want Nothing + Do Anything = Have Everything.* New York: Penguin, 2016.

Resnick, Stella. *The Pleasure Zone: Why We Resist Good Feelings & How to Let Go and Be Happy.* York Beach, ME: Conari Press, 1997.

Richardson, Cheryl. *The Art of Extreme Self-Care: Transform Your Life One Month at a Time.* Carlsbad, CA: Hay House Publishing, 2012.

Sincero, Jen. *You Are a Badass.* Philadelphia: Running Press, 2013.

Smith, Dr. Bob, and Bill Wilson. *The Big Book of Alcoholics Anonymous.* New York: Alcoholics Anonymous World Services, 1939. Reprint 2013.

Thomashauer, Regena. *Mama Gena's School of Womanly Arts: Using the Power of Pleasure to Have Your Way with the World.* New York: Simon & Schuster, 2002.

ACKNOWLEDGMENTS

*T*hanks to my mother, a mom entrepreneur before the term existed, who always said I should be a writer. I wish you were here.

I'm grateful to Shelley Doctors, Jacques Depardieu, Terri Cole, and Terry DeMeo, for gently guiding me toward a better way.

Thanks to Stephanie Krikorian for believing in this project when it was just an idea. Thanks to Linda Sivertsen and my Carmel writing group for teaching me how to be a writer.

Thanks to Anthony Ziccardi and the entire team at Post Hill Press.

Thank you to Maureen Ahern for your positive energy and tireless efforts every day on behalf of our little project, *momAgenda*, that turned into so much more than we ever dreamed. Tom Glazer and Diana Loevy, thank you for helping me turn my idea into a business. Thank you Heather Harris for being part of this team from the beginning, and for taking all my scribbles and doodles and making them beautiful. To all the team members who have helped momAgenda grow into what it is today, thank you.

To every *momAgenda* customer and every member of our wonderful community, thank you for your support.

To my friends, your support, advice, and love have carried me through good times and bad. I'm lucky to have friends from every stage of life that have become sisters. Lara, Angelica, Heidi, Laura, Julie, Aubrey, Leslie, Lori, Julia, Lisa, Katrina, Elizabeth, everyone in my Colgate crew, and the extraordinary women in my beloved feminine movement tribe, thank you for being you.

I'm grateful to my kids, Andrew, Jenna, Matthew, and Jamie, for being amazing humans that make me proud every day. I'm extraordinarily fortunate to have a happy blended family—thank you Larry and Tara Restieri, and Megan and Molly Bugniazet. Thank you to my sister, Liz, and brother, Charlie, who are always there for me. To my aunts Marie and Pam and my cousins, especially Jen, Nancy, and Annie, whose love and support over the years helped me more than I can say—I couldn't have done it without you. My mother always told me family is the most important thing. I'm glad that, on this point at least, I listened.

Author photo by Lori Berkowitz

About the Author

Nina Restieri is the founder and president of momAgenda. Previously, she has spent time as an advertising executive, as the president of a family business, and as a stay-at-home mom. She started momAgenda when her four kids were seven, five, three, and one, to create organizing products to help make moms' lives (and her own life) easier. momAgenda has grown to include a diversified range of products that help organize the lives of mothers and others, including day planners, home organizers, pads, journals, and accessories. The collection is sold at leading national retailers and regional boutiques throughout the U.S. Over the past fifteen years, Nina Restieri and momAgenda have been featured in numerous outlets including NBC's *Today* show, *The Early Show*, MSNBC, *Real Simple*, *Better Homes and Gardens*, *The New York Times*, and *The Huffington Post*.

Nina lives in Connecticut with her four children. This is her first book.